Special Praise for *Don't Be a Dick*

"If you had to design the perfect person to tell you how NOT to be a dick, Mark's the guy. I know Mark as a friend, author, contributor, spouse (not mine), parent, surfer dude, and fellow opera-lover, and I can assure you that Mark is the anti-dick. He's also witty and knowledgeable. Don't be a dick—buy this book."

—Hara Estroff Marano, author of *A Nation of Wimps*, editor at large for *Psychology Today*

"*Don't Be a Dick: Change Yourself, Change Your World* is a fabulous book that truly is your journey to freedom and happiness! Mark focuses on the key secret that makes twelve-step programs into miraculous crucibles of transformation: Do not harbor or act out of resentment—no matter what someone else has done or not done to set you off. If you do harbor resentment, you, yourself, will suffer. This is a hard truth to grasp, but Mark shows us exactly how it works. And most importantly he shows us how to shed the poison of resentment and rise above it to right action, serenity, and miraculous breakthroughs."

—Diana Kirschner, PhD, international bestselling author of *Love in 90 Days*

"In *Don't Be a Dick*, Mark shows us how to transform the 'adversarial' world into a place of improbable joy and peace by revealing, both to ourselves and to others, the truth about our anxiety and vulnerability."

—Daniel Berry, RN, MHA, coauthor of *Irrelationship* and *Relationship Sanity*

"Borg gets to the problem quickly, hence the title. The solution? Admit, amend, and repeat. Brilliant!"

—John Turi, author of *A Drinker with a Writing Problem*

"Dr. Borg's latest book is a roadmap for change, leading us to a better world. I plan to send his book to all the dicks I know for the holidays! Seriously, it's well-researched, addresses underlying issues that lead to dicky behavior, and provides an easy-to-follow action plan to achieve change. Thank you Dr. Borg for this important book!"

—Tom Shanahan, author of *Spiritual Adrenaline*

"Mark Borg works out what causes us to unleash our inner jerk on the world. His expert advice paired with a searing sense of humor gives us the tools to deal with self-destructive, 'us vs. them' behaviors once and for all. We all need this book. It really could change the world."

—Dana Bowman, author of *Bottled* and
How to Be Perfect Like Me

Don't Be a Dick

DON'T BE A DICK

CHANGE YOURSELF, CHANGE YOUR WORLD

MARK B. BORG, Jr.

CENTRAL RECOVERY PRESS

LAS VEGAS

Central Recovery Press (CRP) is committed to publishing exceptional materials addressing addiction treatment, recovery, and behavioral healthcare topics.

For more information, visit www.centralrecoverypress.com.

Publisher: Central Recovery Press
              3321 N. Buffalo Drive
              Las Vegas, NV 89129

24 23 22 21 20 19   1 2 3 4 5

Library of Congress Cataloging-in-Publication Data

Names: Borg, Mark B., Jr., author.
Title: Don't be a dick : change yourself, change your world / Mark B. Borg,
    Jr., PhD.
Description: Las Vegas, NV : Central Recovery Press, [2019]
Identifiers: LCCN 2019010637 (print) | LCCN 2019012799 (ebook) | ISBN
    9781949481037 (ebook) | ISBN 9781949481020 (pbk. : alk. paper)
Subjects: LCSH: Change (Psychology) | Interpersonal conflict. | Behavior
    modification.
Classification: LCC BF637.C4 (ebook) | LCC BF637.C4 B673 2019 (print) | DDC
    155.2/4--dc23
LC record available at https://lccn.loc.gov/2019010637

Photo of Mark B. Borg, Jr. by Lisa Ross at Studio Lisa Ross
Every attempt has been made to contact copyright holders. If copyright holders have not been properly acknowledged, please contact us. Central Recovery Press will be happy to rectify the omission in future printings of this book.

Publisher's Note: This book contains general information about relationships, recovery, and related matters. The information is not medical advice. This book is not an alternative to medical advice from your doctor or other professional healthcare provider.

Our books represent the experiences and opinions of their authors only. Every effort has been made to ensure that events, institutions, and statistics presented in our books as facts are accurate and up-to-date. To protect their privacy, the names of some of the people, places, and institutions in this book may have been changed.

Cover design by The Book Designers
Interior design and layout by Sara Streifel, Think Creative Design

A long time ago someone left me a mean voicemail, saying, "You've got John. You've got Jim. You've got Bill. And that's *it!*" It was true then, and still is. The caller was referring to my short list of soul mates—dudes with whom I've walked in love for decades. John "Purple" Turi, Jim DeLozier of All Nite Rave, and Bill Zunkel. Add to that list Chris Borg, Mike Dalla, Kristy Matthews, and Danny Berry. These people offer the kind of love that allows me to resist the siren song of dickery. Their love is a cornerstone for all of my endeavors. It's the very foundation that challenges, encourages, and supports me as I strive every day to be a loving and caring husband, father, child, psychoanalyst, author, and friend. This book is both inspired by and dedicated to y'all.

TABLE OF CONTENTS

Part IV: Dicks in Recovery

Being a Dick Is the Self-Destruct Button

You walk into your shrink's office and say, "Whenever I say 'F— you' to someone, I put myself in a position to be hurt. The bad feeling I want to project onto someone else is happening to me."

"In other words," replies your shrink, "whenever you say 'F— you,' you're really saying, 'F— *me*.'"

We all carry around more than our fair share of unexpressed anger. Yet acting like a dick makes you the unintentional target of other people's hurt, fear, anger, and potential rage, which would otherwise be choked down. The repressed emotions that someone else carries around will have a convenient expression: blasting you. It's that person, then, who inhabits the dick role.

Dickery is synonymous with righteousness, so we experience someone else's reaction to it as an attack. But really, we're being counterattacked. Anyone at any time can slip into dickery simply by believing the anger they feel toward another person is warranted, leading to their choice version of "F— you," which is sometimes saying exactly that. Regardless of gender, race, religion, political affiliation, or what have you, we are all similar in this way. Our bad behavior unintentionally triggers counter-reactions from others, and we use their counter-reactions to *retroactively* justify our righteously indignant, dickish attitude. This cycle of behavior causes us to misinterpret counterattacks as unprovoked attacks. In essence, we victimize ourselves through our own dickery.

It's a miserable way to live. I've helped many people work through this and all that underlies it. I can help you, too!

The best way to protect ourselves from dicks is to not be one ourselves. Our experience of the world, beginning with our earliest interactions with our primary caretakers, influences the way we interact with other people. If we can understand those moments when the world—or rather, some person in it—provokes us to act like a dick and navigate our way through such moments with awareness, we can, as the Buddha says, learn that our troubles are our best teachers. Our troubles—especially those we invite in through dickery—can teach us:

- How we've protected ourselves through dickish behavior

- How we've invited dickish counterattacks

- How to halt our defensiveness and live at peace with others

- That we can positively influence other's reactions and responses to us

- That this transformative process can change the world

I've amassed immense personal and professional experience that convinces me beyond measure that being a dick is a form of self-punishment. As dicks, we either isolate ourselves from personal connections or set ourselves up as roving punching bags. Trending literature is full of advice for people who need to protect themselves from dicks, especially narcissists, sociopaths, and psychopaths. My work in academia, as well as self-help and pop-psych publishing also gives me plenty of expertise in this area. However, I've found that the best "classroom," and what ultimately authorizes me to pen this book, has been my collaboration with other authors, academics, and clinicians. Business relationships are often prone to conflict. I once struggled to not blow up a much-cherished, multi-year project with colleagues I cared for deeply (and still do!). Since I didn't want to lose their friendship, our professional relationships, or the project itself I told myself: *Don't be a dick*. Writing this book served as a pause for me, an opportunity to calm down and develop constructive, thoughtful responses (as opposed to impulsive, destructive reactions) to any crisis at hand.

One thing I learned was that sometimes just repeating the mantra *don't be a dick* offers the most essential tool—a pause button. So, I invite you to use this book to avoid your own knee-jerk reactions to the muck life throws at you. Let's take this chance to not be dicks—together!

The lesson of all dickery is writ large here; the fight against external dickery (that which we perceive in others) sooner or later turns into a fight against our inner dick (the one we're tempted to be).

This book's solutions are founded upon the premise mentioned earlier that the best way to avoid meeting a dick is to not be one yourself. How do we do this? The simplest way to put it is *never hurt, always help*.

INTRODUCTION

Saying Hello

You receive an accusatory text message from an important colleague at 5:30 a.m. on a Monday morning. She's angry, the message being that you messed things up again. In this moment you have two choices. An immediate defensive reaction can instantly unravel a patiently and thoughtfully constructed business relationship that has flourished for years. But telling her how annoyed you feel would be *oh so satisfying*. So, do you:

1. React defensively, like a dick? Or,

2. Hit pause, toss and turn a bit, go back to sleep, wake up, and craft a measured, non-defensive reply that accounts for your colleague's thoughts, feelings, and potentially valid points?

If option 2 has *not* been your approach historically, this book is for you.

Maybe you thought being a dick was a gendered behavior,[1] something relegated to hormone-driven boys playing grab ass in high school locker rooms. While not untrue, this is certainly not the whole story. I've met plenty of women who are dicks and I'm sure you have as well. Mostly, being a dick—a douchebag, an asshole, a blowhard— is a dramatic reaction that leads to treating people poorly. Yet at its core, being a dick is a cover-up for our own vulnerability. We act out due to an inability to accept circumstances as they are—a resistance to living life on life's terms. What we do is scapegoat ourselves, in a sense, by attracting blame for the flawed system that raised us to be afraid of human connection. We act like dicks, which then leads to a savage, polarizing state of Us vs. Them, them being everyone else. Examples of this are when we:

- Blame someone else for everything that goes wrong in a relationship, as dicks do

- Accept full responsibility ourselves for what in truth is a "takes two to tango" situation, which makes us feel like victims and sets us up for future reactive dickery

Both tactics invite dickery to further enter and entrench itself into our relationships.[2] In this sense, being a dick is like a defensive puffing up that masks what we really need from others and truly feel about ourselves. And absolutely *anyone* under the right circumstances can be a dick.

Being a clinical psychologist and psychoanalyst is my day job, and from that realm I can assure you there is no formal diagnosis for being a dick, or for the associated constellation of symptoms that manifest as what I call dickery. Yet, still, I cannot tell you how many of the problems I treat clinically and therapeutically have to do with my clients acting like dicks, being mistreated by other dicks, or some combination of the two. In fact, I've found it's often a cyclical, ever-shifting dynamic whereby a person perpetrates dickery in one instant and is the victim the next.

It can be tempting to attribute being a dick to circumstances such as city living. In the twenty years I've lived in New York, I've recognized times in which there was some positive benefit to acting like a dick; I felt like I righted some terrible injustice, for example. But these were always short-term gains and usually resembled reactions to my own insecurities. In this sense, being a dick amounts to a survival tactic. However, the more I've explored this behavior, the more I see it as an epidemic condition. In fact, rather than a tactic or skill, being a dick is often the biggest mistake people make, and they make it every day. Romance, finance, parenthood, and work life are all fertile grounds for dickery. It's my belief—hard-earned through the painful experiences of many clients, couples, families, communities, organizations, and my own life—that there's no quicker way to make life difficult than by being a dick.

This book is for anyone who notices that their behavior tends to backfire, leaving them feeling alone and uncertain as to why their seemingly warranted behavior consistently has poor results. If you're constantly using the refrain, "It's not me, it's them," whenever something goes wrong, I'm here to tell you that it is, in fact, you. But that's good news; if these troubles are your fault then there's something you can do to reverse the behaviors that cause them and enjoy a happy, fulfilling life. You may have bought this book for someone else, but it turns out you're the one who needs it!

Forget the Narcissist. It's Really about You

One pervasive focus in therapeutic and lay psychology is narcissism as a trait we should protect ourselves from at all costs. The "Most Popular" blog post on PsychologyToday.com is almost always a list of characteristics associated with narcissists, sociopaths, psychopaths, or bullies, along with tips to guard against such persons. The downside of this advice is that persistently anticipating these types of people, and rigorously protecting ourselves from their notorious behavior, leads to a state of constant anxiety. This may trigger our own dickish behavior, as we preemptively overprotect ourselves.

What if, as an alternative, we turn the approach on its head? Using the recovery philosophy of "keeping the focus on ourselves" is a powerful way to do just that. In the twelve-step recovery program, Step Four, "made a fearless and searching moral inventory of ourselves," and Step Ten, "continued to take personal inventory, and when we were wrong promptly admitted it," recommend this sense of self-awareness. It's not that we need to avoid narcissists; we have to work to not add fuel to their fire, and as a result decrease our target potential. So, to protect yourself from narcissistic dicks, avoid joining their parade. As you'll learn, the secret of any relationship is to turn off your finely-tuned ability to sniff out, detect, and confront others' bad behavior. That sort of social policing is also an example of bad behavior. It's also the equivalent of putting on a "kick me" sign, because when we confront dickery with dickery, the results are ugly.

To solve the problems dicks bring on and make this a happier world we needn't obsess about the actions of others. We can't control them. All we have to do is be satisfied with the small sliver of personal autonomy we *do* possess and not be dicks to anyone for any reason whatsoever.

Addressing the ultimate cover-up that is our sensitivity—the "it's not me, it's them" retort—is not only critical for dealing with dicks, but for unlearning the behaviors that cause us to act that way ourselves. It's the challenge of accepting people that pushes our buttons. But this book will show you how to stop reacting to your deep-seated hurt by being abrasive in ways that allow no chance for respite or reparation, and to be mindful of these same behaviors in others. You'll learn responses that leave room for understanding and halt the cycle of one dickish reaction leading to another, ad infinitum.

Underneath our defensiveness lies a fear of being hurt, rejected, and abandoned. However, when willing to work through these anxieties, we are able to:

1. Hit pause long enough to stop acting like a dick and offer a different kind of reaction to the world

2. Understand when our underlying pain and fear about the way the world treats us is due to our own dickish behavior putting us in a position to be hurt

3. Learn to live with the emotional risks involved in intimacy, empathy, vulnerability, and romantic attachment[3]

4. Consciously let go of defensive behavior and deepen connections to the people who matter most to us, joyfully balancing our focus between ourselves and others

5. Live more comfortably in our own skin, accepting others and ourselves as is

Why Recovery Is the Model

Like substance abuse, being a dick is a self-destructive behavior that starts out as a brief moment of relief, but then becomes a problem. I suggest using tools from twelve-step recovery to overcome dickery because its goal of "applying these principles in all our affairs," a quote from *Alcoholics Anonymous*, and the tenet to cease a self-destructive behavior and replace it with social behaviors represent a blueprint to live at peace with the world.

My professional acquaintance with a twelve-step recovery program began in the late 1980s, when I took my adolescent psychiatric clients to A.A. meetings in Newport Beach, California. There, I noticed that people who recover from addiction through a twelve-step program experience changes that go well beyond their target behavior, be it drug use, overeating, codependency, or something else. The result is a *lifestyle* transformation. Recovery from dickery requires a similar transformation, which is why I lean heavily on the basic ingredients of twelve-step recovery:

- A capacity for honesty with oneself about one's behavior

- An openness to seeing the cause-and-effect nature of one's behavior

- A willingness to address the underlying issues that cause the behavior

- An inventory of one's own behavior and its consequences

- Self-accountability

With the awareness that comes from being honest with ourselves and accountable for our actions, we can put down the dickery we've inadvertently used against ourselves, live at peace with the world, and feel comfortable in our own skin.

How This Book Works

My goal is to empower you to accept yourself as you are. Together we'll disrupt your current state of mind and show you the potential you already have to define your life. Begin by reading *Don't Be A Dick* from front to back; each chapter builds upon the next. Make sure you have a journal on hand to collect your insights along the way. Designed as an interactive guidebook, it includes exercises that give you a chance to dive deeper into your personal story, and encourages you to engage in conversation with yourself as you understand more about your relationship to the world, move into recovery, and make tangible changes to your life. You may make entries in your journal chapter-by-chapter, or return to sections of interest later, when you feel moved to write and respond.

Of course, mark up any part of the book that strikes a chord to identify material that resonates with you or mirrors aspects of your experience. I have no doubt you'll experience a number of "aha" moments, and may even enjoy some instant relief as you absorb information, recall anecdotes of people trapped in dickery, and recognize opportunities to launch your recovery. My hope is that you find valuable knowledge, tools, and support that open a door to new ways of living and loving.

The program I've created will teach you to stop the inner game of shame and self-doubt, an internal violence that begets external bullying. When you stop being a dick to yourself, you'll stop treating others that way too. Buddhist philosophy suggests that when we stop the inner war, we can live at peace with ourselves and the world around us. The same teachings can be found in the twelve-step adage, "Hurt people hurt people."

Each chapter delivers the latest research, real world stories, and most importantly, exercises that allow you to explore your own emotional experience to see how you're being a dick in your daily life, who bears the brunt of your anger, and who treated you poorly in the past.

In Part I, you'll learn exactly how you've stepped on the toes of others and why you adopted this behavior pattern in the first place. By parsing through old relationships, you'll bring up the suppressed anxieties that cause you to act like a dick not always, but frequently enough. You also learn the difference between being *right* and being *righteous*, and how the latter is the most limiting behavior dicks carry in their arsenal. Lastly, you'll understand how the myth of cathartic relief—the once popular notion that it's important to let off steam—doesn't serve you in the short run and hinders your ability to have healthy long-term relationships. I'll also show you ways to express conflict without being a bully.

In Part II, you'll learn how to spot a dick from afar and recognize the telltale ploys of their unique dickery. Instead of avoiding them, however (or worse, patrolling their bad behavior), you'll have the skills to deal with difficult or obnoxious people at home and in the office. You'll also see why your closest relationships are the easiest to sabotage, regardless of whether the dickish behavior is yours or theirs.

In Part III, you'll begin the work of recovery. Similar to Step Ten of the traditional twelve-step model, which suggests that we "continue to take personal inventory, and when we were wrong, promptly admitted it," I provide a self-assessment tool that allows you to keep the focus on your dickery and ultimately to change your relationship with the world. You'll learn self-acceptance, to stop being a dick to yourself, and the skills needed to pause your thoughts and actions. The fix is easy: behaviorally, there's not that much to it. The lesson is to think before you speak and, umm, just don't be a dick.

In Part IV, I'll explain why not being a dick may be the key to living a happy, fulfilling life. More simply than that, not being a dick is a milestone on the road to accepting life, ourselves, and each other.

Go Ahead and Say Hello

You know that person you feel slighted by? The one who doesn't say hello at work and hasn't acknowledged you in any of the thirty spin classes you've taken together? She's that person who, even though your kids are pals, never asked if you wanted to arrange a playdate. It's inevitable that you'll be stuck in an elevator with that person someday. But guess what? Everything you think and feel about them is probably awfully similar to what they think and feel about you. So, go ahead and say hello.

You're also bound to run into that guy you think is a dick when you're coming out of the restroom one day. It's written in the stars that he also happens to be your new love interest's close friend. And that woman whose child your kid desperately wants a playdate with? Turns out she thinks you're a dick because several months ago *you* didn't say hi, and now you have to sit next to each other on a playground bench for the foreseeable future.

Some part of you knows that when you smile at this person, when you make the mighty effort to be nice to them, you'll realize they're very kind. *They always are.*

Say hello to that dick who just a minute ago thought the same thing about you.

PART I

STICKING IT TO OURSELVES AND THE WORLD

CHAPTER ONE

What's Being a Dick All About?

A famous Jesuit mystic by the name of Father Anthony de Mello once promoted the brilliant and counterintuitive notion that "everything is okay as is."[4] He believed that with God in our hearts, we're in pretty good hands. It's a fluid theory that I like to apply to a peaceful relationship with the world. We're already okay, we just need to attune ourselves to recognize as much. We spend so much energy operating in ways that ensure that we don't feel okay, and won't in the future. We provoke others to treat us poorly and continually feel awful.

We can ponder, research, and explore the myriad reasons for dickery in others—in fact, philosophy, psychology, and sociology have hypotheses, theories, and answers galore for these questions. Religions imply that it's a sin. Psychology labels it a protective measure against anxiety caused by vulnerability. Philosophy elevates and contorts dickishness into deep questions about the nature of existence. Obviously, attaining insight into *why* is only part of the solution. The real remedy to dickishness is to put insight into action.

That said, it's smart to have a sense of why people act like a dick in the first place.

The unconscious reason is to sideline oneself from full participation in life. When we are unkind to people, they avoid us. Now, how could *that* be the goal? you might ask. The answer is that full engagement is scary, especially when it comes to relationships. So, being a dick allows us to avoid the riskier aspects of feeling connected to people.

Why is that a problem? After all, isn't it wise to avoid situations that feel scary or dangerous? Maybe. But being a dick is not a safe way to be on the sidelines. On the contrary, it feels to others like we've kicked them in the gut, so they react accordingly. The only sidelining going on is that of our emotional connection to these people, places, and things that have overwhelmed us by threatening to matter. Knowing the isolation that being a dick causes, you might consider having more conscious control over how you treat others and how they respond. Ironically, being a dick invites others to yank you off the sidelines with direct emotional engagement in the form of conflict.

While dicks often misread other people's counterattacks as having been unprovoked, if you bought this book (or someone bought it for you), you probably know that you provoke people. Misinterpreting the root cause of others' aggression sets us up for a hostile relationship with the world, and to stop, your perception, attitudes, and actions will have to change. Unkind actions inspire bad attitudes, and bad attitudes fuel unkind actions. Before you know it, both can become features of your character—the essence of how you experience yourself.[5]

Let's look closer at those underlying attitudes that cause you to be a dick.

Why Did You Get so Good at Being Bad?

Most dicks intend for their bad behavior to solve various social problems, especially those associated with being vulnerable, invested in, or close to people who might hurt them. Though not the inevitable outcome, being a dick is also common when you're chronically stewing in resentment over feeling ripped-off, neglected, overlooked, diminished, or devalued. One of my now-sober alcoholic clients said, "Now that I've kicked the drink, *resentment* is my drug of choice."

Where do those feelings come from? Simply put: anxiety. It inundates us when our sense of self contradicts what someone has communicated about us, be it through something they said or how they've treated us. Over time, an internal security system develops— what's called the "self-system"—which minimizes our awareness of anxiety.[6]

Relationships are the primary source of anxiety. It exists on a gradient scale, but is particularly severe in dicks, who've crafted an entire way of life to manage its chilling effects.

We're built to withstand all kinds of anxiety-provoking stimuli, but the real trick is to manage anxiety itself. That means not becoming so overwhelmed we cannot function (i.e., anxiety disorder), and not becoming so defended against it that we don't feel anything at all (as with depression). To pull this off, we guard against anxiety triggers. The mechanisms to block our awareness of anxiety operate along a continuum that stretches from selectively avoiding things that bother us (simply not paying attention) to thoroughly blocking all conscious evidence of an experience having occurred at all. The latter is called *dissociation*. What these strategies have in common is an ability to numb our awareness of anxiety, fear, and pain.

And what becomes of those emotions we don't consciously feel? Well, just because we don't feel the fears doesn't mean we're not affected by them. Or to put it another way, not being aware of how we feel doesn't mean we don't feel. In fact, our behavior toward ourselves and others is generally *more* affected by unconscious feelings than by the ones we're thinking of. And in the long run, feelings demand expression. Whatever it is that we're pushing out of our awareness will eventually find a way through to us, and those around us.

So, being a dick is a psychological strategy to mitigate our experience of anxiety and stress. But as a side effect, our responses don't allow others in who might help remedy the situation. In that way, being a dick isolates us, reinforcing a disconnection from awareness of that which we truly want and need from the world—emotional support. Because being a dick begins as a reaction to a world that feels out of control, assessing our current responses to stress helps us understand the behaviors and patterns that develop around these defensive reactions. The next section presents some of the mechanisms behind your dickish behavior that relate to anxiety.

You Might as Well Blame Your World

Interpersonal psychoanalysts believe we get to know ourselves through "reflected appraisals"[7] of our environment, our relationships, and in particular our early encounters with primary caregivers. One's whole sense of self develops through these appraisals, so in a sense, how people treat us becomes who we are.

When we take an early, unresolved relationship dynamic or conflict into our current relationships, that's called *enactment*.[8] You and I, in the dynamic patterns we use to communicate and interact, reengage in behaviors, thoughts, and feelings that repeat our essential early, unresolved conflict. Basically, our defenses are put into play in important relationships again and again. Our feelings then become *enacted* indefinitely. In new relationships and amongst strangers, we replay the unresolved conflicts and relationship dynamics that caused us to install our defenses in the first place. These enactments aren't limited to our immediate family, or anyone who may have directly hurt us. When it comes to how painful and frightening experiences impact us, we tend to generalize, treating everyone in the world as if they're the source of our hurt and fear.

Dicks work both sides of the field: offense and defense. In fact, those who think of their dickish behavior as defensive still enact it offensively, protecting themselves by attacking, provoking, playing the victim, and doing whatever it takes to knock others off their game to avoid being hurt.

If you're a dick, the likelihood is that you run on obsessive fuel; your anger rationalizes your behavior as you think compulsively about the people who hurt you, and you simultaneously become the target of other's obsessions, since the people you hurt retaliate. Again, all dicks mistake counterattacks for unprovoked attacks. But people trapped in what feels like a threatening emotional experience are not just your average, run-of-the-mill dicks. While they may seem naturally inclined to devalue others, they actually feel like they're fighting for their lives. After all, if someone else's behavior seriously affects how you feel about yourself—that is, threatens your very sense of self—you can be damned sure it's going to trigger you to react as if your very life is at stake.

It's not so hard to see how being a dick serves as a kind of preemptive strike against reflected appraisals—the way we see ourselves in the context of others' treatment. How we experience ourselves influences how we navigate situations that might trigger anxiety, and those unconscious choices can feel like habit rather than reactive decisions. There can even be the sense that how you behave is simply who you are. As if being a dick is so essential, it feels more like fate or heredity than a juvenile defense developed from the perception that the world is scary. We keep acting like dicks to retroactively and preemptively account for other people's bad behavior, all but ensuring that poor treatment indeed comes down on us in a self-fulfilling prophecy.

It's Not You, It's Me

Dicks attract ill consequences from the people in their environments. Intentionally behaving rudely allows them to make sense of other people's substandard treatment of them, yet that kind of retroactive excuse-making is often extended to the people who were unwilling or unable to effectively care for them as kids as well. Dicks are inclined to believe that it wasn't the caretaker's fault, it was *theirs*. Acting out at a young age might have started as a protest against being treated poorly, but it winds up as resignation. A young dick might also be mimicking the bad behavior of their caretakers.

You might have turned the tables on your poor caretakers. But now your bad behavior—not their poor parenting—is the problem. In this process, you let them off the hook for not providing appropriate care. "It was all me," says the regretful dick. "I deserved to be hit. I brought it upon myself." Or: "Why would anyone have looked out for me? I was a terror." In this way, we justify a state of isolated self-sufficiency, overlook the impact of others' behaviors, and continue to give everyone a pass for never giving us what we want or need.

It takes great empathy to forgive others for dropping the ball and deem their actions humane instead of a form of assault. But truthfully, being a dick doesn't allow for that kind of empathy to develop; we can't accept others, nor they us, in all of our fallible, sometimes not-very-nice humanness, so the conflict continues.

Seeing What I Can't Stand in Me, in You

Seeing what you can't stand—what you downright hate—about yourself reflected in others is among the most primitive and common psychological defenses. It's called *projection*, and like all psychological defenses, it's a survival mechanism. We mitigate anxieties simply to function. But for dicks, this reaction can be disastrous.

Say you're walking down a busy city street and your blood begins to boil as you dodge and weave between all those people happily nodding their heads along with whatever music is playing in their ear buds as they type on their phones. You start mumbling and giving them dirty looks. You call someone a jerk. You tell yourself all these people are entitled, selfish, narcissistic assholes who, when they come close to running into you, don't deserve to live. You stop in front of one or two of them and they actually bump right into you, mumble something—"sorry," maybe—and move along. You're just about to punch the next person who bumps into you when your cell phone buzzes. You get a message that you promptly begin to reply to as you weave through pedestrian traffic.

What happened? Clearly, other people's bad behavior worked to fuel your own. You started name-calling, you got physically aggressive, you were convinced that everyone else was in the wrong. And perhaps they were, right up until the time when you were the asshole. But whether or not that was dickish behavior is beside the point. The point is that we see unacceptable qualities in others as a defense against acknowledging and doing something about our own. When we use projection and see our horrible qualities in others, our dickishness gets rationalized in a way that makes it very hard to register. This makes it difficult to change. In fact, sometimes we'll only see it when some other person stops in front of us when we're the ones texting on a crowded street. But nah, we won't see it then either. In that case, it's that other person who's the dick, right?

Sounds pretty rough, huh? It sure can be. And that's why people in relationships with dicks project their own bad qualities onto their partners. These tend to be people who:

1. Were born into poor treatment, and hence built a tolerance for other people's dickery, believing the things being projected were true, as in *I really am a 'bad person'*

2. Were raised by people who blamed themselves and their child-rearing skills when problems arose with their children. By claiming failure, they become scapegoats for their child's belief in what was wrong with him or herself

3. Don't see the poor treatment they receive coming, and due perhaps to unresolved dynamic issues, believe they can handle anything. This person tends to absorb the burden of perceived wrongs and is often a rescuer-type who seeks out "lost causes," another category of dick

4. Believe it is their job to help dicks, even if that entails getting cornered and having their ass kicked psychologically

That's just the short list of people attracted to dicks. Family members, lovers, and therapists tend to be the best receptacles for projections of what we despise about ourselves. We often see character defects in others more easily than we do in ourselves. Combined with our compulsion to repeat old, unresolved dynamic patterns in current relationships—our enactments—this blindness to our flaws makes our relationships hotbeds for projections run amok.

The good news is that when we're honest about how our issues complicate our lives and lead to problems in our relationships, the urge to project onto others diminishes. When we feel safe with others, we recognize that our dickery corresponds with qualities we've been unable to face in ourselves. On the other hand, if we never accept responsibility for the character defects we project onto others, we risk walking through life unaware that other people are not the problem—we are. That is very bad news, because there's nothing we can do about the problem if it's not us.

Sometimes owning up to our dissociated and denied self-experience obstructs how we need to see ourselves. For instance, Jerry was brutalized as a child, and rather than see himself as an abused person, he sees himself as someone who can take and deliver a punch. He won't allow himself to remember how unsafe and vulnerable he was; instead he sees himself as "tough" for overcoming early pain and difficulty. He needs to see himself this way; it's how he survived. Whatever it is that we're blocking can be serious. For people who've been traumatized, their off-putting behavior may be meant to thwart relationships that cause them to reexperience old pain and fear.

Someone who was badly hurt in early life, like Jerry, can be triggered into highly self-protective behaviors by relationships that make them feel vulnerable. In fact, in Jerry's last relationship, when he started to feel safe enough to open up, he saw his partner as "weak" and left her. He had identified in her what he most deeply feared and could not accept in himself.

It's a Black and White World

In the earliest stages of development, the mind categorizes things that we depend on, from food to caretakers, as being all good or all bad. It's a primitive way to manage anxiety and aggression; splitting objects into either/or boxes provides a basic sense of where bad stuff comes from and allows us to believe that bad things in the world (and ourselves) can be contained. The all-good/all-bad lens is called the *paranoid-schizoid position*.[9] In this state the split between all-good and all-bad is so extreme, we quite literally experience things—say, Dad—as good objects in one instance, bad objects in another. It feels like Dad is two totally separate beings, since his bad side is so intolerable to us. We have the rationale we need then to be a dick.

A significant developmental step occurs when you experience the same person—a key caregiver like a mother, for instance—as no longer all bad or all good, but rather a modicum of both. This state is referred to as the *depressive position*. If we can reach this position in which we accept gray areas in our lives, each other, and ourselves, we can think differently about our hostility. For example, if being a dick is your way to protect yourself, it might help to learn that this attitude and behavior is not a permanent part of your character, but a misstep in your development that can be repaired. If you put your weapons down, you'll likely see the world do the same. Perhaps in this way we reconcile with the world, one relationship at a time.

Unfortunately, most people caught in dickish routines have no inkling that anything is wrong until it stops working in their favor, despite having seemed to work well in the past. Our acting-out behaviors so effectively distract us from anxiety, we can't imagine anything needs changing. We have no idea how afraid we are. And this unconscious fear of being vulnerable disallows change of any kind. Equally destructive is the possibility that our underlying fear drives us to change quickly, compulsively, and unreflectively, without allowing a new situation to prove worthwhile.

What Does It Mean to Act Out?

Once you can see what drives your behavior, the next step is to see how it manifests in you acting like a dick. In the realm of psychotherapy and analysis, the term *acting out* refers to any behavior that serves as a "substitute for remembering past events."[10] We sometimes act like dicks to suppress unpleasant memories, which may include experiences of trauma. In his seminal paper, "Remembering, Repeating, and Working Through," Sigmund Freud introduced the concepts of the *repetition compulsion* and offered a systematic definition for acting out. Pointing to the relationship between memory and repetition, Freud wrote: "The patient does not remember anything of what he has forgotten and repressed but acts it out. He reproduces it not as a memory but as an action; he repeats it, without, of course, knowing that he is repeating it ... he cannot escape from the compulsion to repeat; and in the end we understand that this is his way of remembering."[11]

Freud went on to introduce the term *agieren* to describe what happened when a client named Dora prematurely ended her treatment. He stated: "Because of the unknown quantity in me which reminded Dora of Herr K., she took her revenge on me as she wanted to take her revenge on him . . . Thus she acted out an essential part of her recollections and phantasies instead of producing it in the treatment."[12]

The psychoanalyst Jacques Lacan believed acting out to be a demand for recognition.[13] For our purposes, the term will describe any behavior that lets an intolerable emotion to bypass our conscious awareness. As I've stated before, though, we do not eradicate intolerable emotions, only our *awareness* of them. This means the bad feelings we have about ourselves remain intact even when our behavior effectively gets rid of our conscious awareness of them.

It's a vicious circle; the more you dislike yourself, the more you act out to eradicate that feeling. You behave like a dick, causing other people to treat you poorly or avoid you entirely. And this goes on *ad infinitum*.

It's not just that we don't *want* to see or accept bad feelings about ourselves; we are *driven* to get rid of them.

Cultural theorist Slavoj Žižek presents a brilliant example of the difference between this desire and drive in his book, *The Parallax View*.[14] Describing a little girl who tries to grab a bright red ball, he explains that she wants the ball—capturing the ball is her goal—but her hands are small and the ball is big, so when she reaches for it, the ball slips away. Her desire leads her to chase it around the room, and at some point, her goal having been frustrated many times over, yet still having fun nonetheless, her desire transforms. Giggling as she chases the ball all over the place, she becomes interested in *sustaining* the process. Now, instead of wishing to capture the ball, she is driven to *not* capture it in order to keep the game going. Drive is not permanently connected to a specific goal. In this example, the situation demands that the little girl *forget* her original desire. The goal of drive can be to *miss its mark*, making it a powerful underlying force to sustain bad behavior and block awareness of anxiety.

For instance, when Erica's fiancé cancelled their engagement she became what she calls a "serial dater." Erica, an attractive, second-generation Chinese-American, grew up with a single mother who had been abandoned by her husband, Erica's father, when they reached New York. Erica is now a successful entrepreneur with an MBA from a prestigious university. At first, she thought she was just having fun and getting over her ex. But what she really wanted was to get rid of her horrible feelings of rejection and abandonment. She had dated her ex, Ryan, since college, so she had in some ways lost sight of how men responded to her. In what became an increasingly *driven* process, she chewed up and spit out the men who pursued her. It was not simple naiveté that led her suitors through her dating game. Initially she would claim a genuine interest in the would-be lover. She was acting out a need to be wanted, longed for, and recognized. But beneath her awareness, these experiences triggered hurt and fear, and prompted a need for revenge against the same category of person who had hurt her.

It initially seemed like Erica was reenacting the emotions of her jilted mother, yet Erica now inhabits the role of her fearful father, the dick.

If by acting out you relive a past need for recognition from others, you're doomed to repeat this most crucial emotional conflict in new relationships. Amazingly, we seem to not want to experience the parts of ourselves that we defend against, and in avoiding these feelings, often wind up missing essential knowledge of who we are. Crucial aspects of our self-experience are covered up.

Dickishness driven by the need to *not feel* blocks self-awareness, self-acceptance, and self-love. It's a highly effective way to distort an intolerable truth. But being a dick also defends us against things we truly want, such as being accepted, liked, and cared for by others. If we let go of our acting-out behavior, we will be confronted by truths that are so difficult to bear that our minds have gone to extreme lengths to hide them. Connecting our dickery to the past and present contexts in which it was born may be scary at first, but in so doing, we can experience a broader emotional life.

So, let's give ourselves a chance to make some connections between our dickish behavior, thoughts, feelings, and general experience of ourselves.

The Dick Quiz

Being a dick is like that grade-school joke: he who smelt it, dealt it. Setting aside the zillion ways one can act out, there's only one surefire way to know you're a dick: you encounter them everywhere.

Are you one of those people who bought this book to help you deal with the other dicks in your life? Like an increasingly bothersome husband or a pesky roommate? If so, it may be worth considering whether *you're* the dick in this dynamic. If so, you're probably screaming "screw this checklist" right now. Still, I have to ask, do you:

- Feel like you're getting one over, tricking the world?

- Feel threatened by others and the world?

- Experience the world as a scary place?

- Feel anxious both when alone or with others?

- Act defensively?

- Feel righteous?

- Believe it's your job to right wrongs?

- Feel compelled to devalue others and put them down?

- Want to be left alone, then suffer from isolation and sadness?

- Feel out of control to the point where you knee-jerk react?

- Feel chronically hurt and angry?

- Lash out easily, but rarely feel bad about it?

- Act adversarial with others and yourself?

- Feel entitled and resentful?

- Say or think epithets like "screw you"?

- Feel uncomfortable with intimacy?

- Hide insecurities and shame?

- Exaggerate accomplishments and take credit for things you haven't really done?

- Act (feel) more important than others?

- Believe you can achieve power through your unique relationship to beauty, success, and intelligence?

- Believe you're so smart and unique that only the best institutions and the most elite professionals can possibly understand you?

- Have an excessive need to be admired all the time?

- Have a sense of entitlement and expect to be treated differently, and with more status, than others?

- Exploit others to get what you want or need?

- Lack empathy and rarely notice what others feel or need? (Genuine empathy is having concern for others without an agenda for yourself.)

- Become jealous and competitive with others or believe that others are jealous of you?

- Become haughty and act arrogant and superior to friends, colleagues, and family?

If you answered yes to some of the above questions, you might be a dick. Checked off more than five and you're likely a colossal dick because, come on, none of these attributes suggest a person who plays well with others!

"Dick" may or may not be a meaningful word to describe yourself, so let's do an exercise to find other words that make sense of how you see yourself as we create a softer world to live in together.

Understanding the "Impletive"

When it comes to being a dick, there's a twist: all the poor behavior we perpetrate upon others likely reflects the way we also mistreat ourselves. It's a screwed-up reversal of *I'm rubber, you're glue, whatever you say bounces off me and sticks to you.* Without realizing it, we talk down to and bully ourselves in ways that match the torment we wreak upon others. This being the case, it's important to work through and let go of the ways we denigrate ourselves.

Negative self-talk impacts how we see and feel about ourselves in ways we barely notice, much less register. When we call ourselves "stupid," or a "dick," what becomes of that? It's the same weaponizing of language that we use against others who hurt or offend us. Do we really think those words will have a different effect against ourselves? Probably not. So, we need to become more thoughtful, careful, and gentle with what we say to ourselves.

When I see #@!&*% on a printed page, as I often do in dialogue bubbles in comics or graphic novels when one character uses an epithet, I choose to read it as a substitute for the word *dick*. (After all, a *dick* is what I tell myself not to be.) The English language contains plenty of words that can stand in for "dick" (admittedly offensive to many people, including my parents). I could've use the word "jerk," but for the behavioral dynamic I'm addressing in this book, I wanted a word with *oomph*. Now that we've got it, though, I want to dial things down. To be gentler to ourselves, let's come up with alternative terms that coincide with our recovery. Coming up with your own expletive is part of the creative process.

You can put your substitute in your head whenever you feel like someone is acting like a dick. Though the point of your #@!% may be to thoughtfully lessen the degree of provocation likely triggered by an expletive like "dick," (it also lessens the offensiveness to my mom and her church friends) any word can refer to the kind of person who, shall we say, *does not play well with others.*

Since "dick" is what we call an expletive, I'll use the word *impletive* to refer to the bleeped-out version you may prefer. Though friends have suggested other names (the #@!% is commonly referred to as a *grawlix,* and other terms I've heard include profanitypes, obscenicons, and redactions), I offer *impletive* because it is an *implied expletive.* As such, it allows each of us to make clear, definitive, indubitable, and explicit as possible our term for a person at war with the world as well as with him or herself.

The transition from impletive (#@!%) to expletive (mine's "dick") will allow you to bring your #@!%-ery out of the shadows and analyze the way it sustains an anxiety-fueled, painful, and scary relationship with the world, and unknowingly places you in a position to be hurt every day.

Without overthinking it, write down a word to describe people, or yourself, when acting out:

1. _____

Just for good measure, add two more:

2. _____

3. _____

Recognizing Internal Agreements

We all engage in unacceptable behaviors. These are unconscious commitments that come out as knee-jerk, cause-and-effect reactions. They tend to be anticipatory, like a life hack to deal with dread over future events, and are reasoned by if/then statements (if you do this then I'm allowed to do that) or ultimatums (I'll end things if I don't get my way).

I call these "agreements" because they guide our behavior in ways that justify being a dick and become acceptable to us over time. For instance, if someone cycles the wrong way in a bike lane I'm entitled to curse at them. Or if someone cuts in front of me in line I have the right to shove them away. These agreements usually result in a highly defensive state of being in the world; we believe we're proactively protecting ourselves from being mistreated, but are actually placing a target on our forehead. In this way, the motto of a dick is always, "The best defense is a good offense."

The problem is that these agreements are exceptionally hard to recognize or do anything about. We've likely been seeing them in everyday life: negative responses, actions, facial expressions, and rude treatment from others who are being dicks around us. But we don't notice when we implement, and in turn invite, those behaviors ourselves.

Agreements developed early in life become a natural part of your character. In fact, as I like to say, your character is the sum total of your psychological defenses;[15] each person's concept of "me" is their most contemporary, up-to-date record of everything they've been through and everything that's been done to them. It's their reaction to all the people who hurt, scared, loved, and cared for them, an immensely complicated history summarized by the simple catchall "me."

Since these agreements have been developing for years, they're stable, sturdy, and not at all easy to change. A sense of safety is essential to change one's nature, making giving up a defensive strategy in a difficult, often dangerous world a big ask. I'm not suggesting you put down all your weapons at once. But through assessment and understanding, I believe disarmament is possible, and as hard as this might be to swallow, doing so will allow you to feel safer in the long run.

In New York, examples of this are innumerable. There's hardly a day that someone doesn't come into my office discussing some infraction perpetrated upon them by some other sidewalk walker, subway rider, driver, or bicyclist (we'll cover this more thoroughly in the Patrolling Dickery chapter). A lot of New Yorkers have the same pet peeves: people walking too slow, people eating smelly food on the subway, people cycling the wrong way in a bike lane. I also find that most of us have "agreements" to excuse our own bad reactions. An agreement may be as mild as *When someone comes charging onto the subway before I exit I'll complain under my breath* to the more serious *If someone bumps me, I'll slap them.* Agreements with ourselves often resemble if/then statements. We're often unaware of them, despite their potential to trigger severe righteousness and justify all kinds of outlandish dickery.

Some agreements are more interpersonal. When I met my client Naomi, she told me, "My girlfriend Gigi likes to ask serious questions about our relationship at night, after turning out the light, when I'm eager to fall asleep. So, given what you've asked me to consider about my personal 'agreements,' I can see that mine relate to a need to wind down before bed—not get worked up in a heavy conversation when I'm trying to fall asleep.

"The agreement is that if Gigi starts discussions about our relationship late at night, I'll politely let her know that, though I'm interested in what she has to say, I need to sleep, so now is not the time. That's the agreement I *want* to have, the one that works for both of us when I'm in a good headspace. But when I'm not, when I'm groggy and exhausted, my agreement becomes: If you mess with me, I will snap, complain, or be dismissive even though you have important concerns you need to air. In this version of the agreement, I'm angry, she's upset, and no one is sleeping well that night."

We tend to make two kinds of agreements:

1. Ones we consciously make when in a good place

2. And ones we unconsciously make when we're not

It's quite possible that unless we've reflected on our agreements, we don't know they exist. And even if we do, we may not spend much time looking at the differences between ones we think we have with, say, our partners, and the ones we actually exhibit. If we gain awareness of our most deep-seated agreements and halt their worst manifestations, our world will change. Your primary task then is to understand your existing agreements and renovate their expressions.

EXERCISE: AGREEMENTS

Agreement	How this agreement plays out in my relationships	The long-term impact on how I relate to others
Example A: Since I'm the only one who provides decent care in the relationship, I won't allow others to contribute to my well-being.	One of us feels burdened and resentful, while the other feels rejected and devalued.	No one I'm involved with seems invested in dealing with problems that arise, so I act out to avoid getting close to others.

CONTINUED ON NEXT PAGE

Agreement	How this agreement plays out in my relationships	The long-term impact on how I relate to others
Example B: I accept whatever others offer me, whether it's what I really want or not, but stew in resentment and feel ignored and hurt afterward.	I feel misunderstood and cannot imagine staying with my partner long-term, though for some reason I've been unable to leave.	I sense my partner doesn't value me, so I quietly resist accepting what he does for me, just like he refuses everything I offer him.

Now, using the above examples as a reference, write down one or two of the agreements you've made with the world. Then think about the following:

- What do your agreements suggest about how you use attitudes and actions to guard against other people?

- How rigid are these agreements, and the attitudes and actions that go with them?

- Is it possible these agreements have put you in a position to be hurt?

- How malleable, given what you've learned so far, might these agreements be?

- Can the transformation we seek come from changing these existing agreements between us and the world? What might that look like?

Dickery as a Relationship with the World

Being a dick puts us into a destructive relationship with the world. But we'll learn to understand and address how being a dick is something that happens between ourselves and others, rather than something that happens solely within one's self. Our "inner dick" suggests bad behavior. But it's our "outer dick" that expresses it and manifests in toxic relationships with the world.

Dicks abound. We can be affected by them directly, as with a spouse, family member, colleague, or boss, or indirectly, when they're politicians, administrators, insurance companies, law enforcement, or other institutions. All of these—be they humans or organizations—are in relationships with us. And without our realizing it, the relationships act as mirrors, reflecting our sense of self-worth.

CHAPTER TWO

Righteous Dickery: It's You Against the World

Above all, dicks are invested in maintaining self-righteousness—the shield in their me-against-the-world battle royale. They go to great lengths to ensure the status quo—their ability to act out rather than consciously process their anxiety—survives every encounter. Dicks isolate from others by embracing a sense of victimhood in a world that's out to get them. It's a form of anxious self-sufficiency. Dicks rely on ever-increasing righteousness to justify their alienating and isolating behavior.

This psychological self-defense, like other "dynamic systems," operates according to the principle of homeostasis, a tendency to return to the average state of expectable functioning, or *regress to the mean*.[16] The "mean" for the dick is when their hostile reactions to the world are justified by the perceived hostility of others. Once a mean is established, no matter how stifling or destructive, it's difficult to break.

The point of this chapter is to assess what fuels your dickery. A wonderful quote from *Alcoholics Anonymous* addresses this sense that, though our anger feels justified, we've wrongly ignored how we trigger aggression in the world:

> *Driven by a hundred forms of fear, self-delusion, self-seeking, and self-pity, we step on the toes of our fellows and they retaliate. Sometimes they hurt us, seemingly without provocation, but we invariably find that at some time in the past we have made decisions based on self which later placed us in a position to be hurt.*[17]

This quote homes in on how we convince ourselves it's "me against the world." When we cannot see our part in a problem, naturally we feel under attack.

The Turd Hurler

Brad and Joe run a small publishing company. They were good friends before they became business partners, and things went well for the first few years. Then Brad's wife became pregnant, and he has struggled to manage the stress.

"Put the money into *that* account," Brad told Joe in a voicemail. The order sounded like a bark through Joe's cell phone. It was 1:00 p.m. on a beautiful Sunday afternoon. It also happened to be Father's Day.

There are innumerable ways to be a weapon against the world, and lobbing poop into someone else's happy day is a perfect example of how mundane and covert being a dick can be, especially when using victimhood as the impetus.

Joe's response was a deliberate silence. He deleted the message and went about his day, knowing that when you attempt to intervene in someone else's dickery, often there are suddenly two dicks in the room. Brad's temper was meant to be dealt with the same way you handle a stray cat: *by not feeding it*. That's the most important lesson in dealing with the turd hurler: *do not engage*. In fact, that's why the term "turd" applies. Once you engage with this person's miserable victimhood, you get it all over you, and it becomes impossible to distinguish whose mess it is. Which stinks.

By way of context, Joe knew his friend felt conflicted about being a father. Joe was also aware that Brad and his equally careerist wife had once all but pricked their fingers and signed an agreement in blood not to have kids. Brad's wife breached the unwritten contract, using threats of divorce and worse as her biological clock ticked on. And of course they had twins.

To turn yourself into a weapon against the world effectively, it helps to know your target. Joe was a dad, too, and fatherhood was among the greatest pleasures in his life, an attitude Brad resented.

In his first marriage, Joe did the exact same thing Brad's wife did. He was the deal-breaker, having realized he wouldn't feel complete until children were a part of his life. Rather than force his wife to contort to his position, however, Joe ended the marriage on near ruinous terms.

Brad knew exactly what kind of mood he was hurling that turd into. And even though it made him look mean, and stirred all kinds of self-pitying, he was willing to hurt himself to upset Joe.

But was Joe hurt? Maybe he would have been a year ago, when Brad first used this tactic. Yet at this point, Joe had distanced himself from that sad, angry person, and all but moved on.

To be sure, things were not going well for Brad. Even though he acquiesced to his wife's need to have children, things had cooled in his marriage, which was not only sexless but loveless, in Brad's eyes. His certainty that *he* was the injured party did not allow him to see how devastated his wife was for having to strongarm him with threats of divorce in order to have kids. Yes, she broke their "agreement." But the dismissive way he treats their children, and even more so how he excuses his dickishness, enrages her. Though Brad's primary grudge was with his wife, that victimhood easily transferred to his business and friendships; anyone who disagreed with Brad on anything whatsoever was wrong. The people he attacked suffered, but of course he hurt himself the most. His wife now hated him, and he and the children, though still under the same roof, were estranged. A head full of self-pity completed Brad's deep sense of victimization.

There is of course plenty wrong with Brad's perspective and the dynamic it ushers in. If someone else is always at fault, he can't do anything to remedy the problem but bully and complain, which, since it's actually unwarranted, compels others to distance themselves. That's what Joe did when he deleted Brad's voicemail.

The most important thing to remember is that the turd hurler will suffer in a state of furious victimhood to punish the world, no matter the cost. The danger is in believing that if you cannot eject a turd hurler from your life, you must *become* one.

There is another way.

Victimhood as a Weapon

One of the most popular narratives in psychology is that we ought to protect ourselves from other people's toxicity—their selfishness, narcissism, and entitlement. But what about protecting ourselves from the ways we sabotage our own happiness and put ourselves in positions to be hurt? Resentment is an emotional toxin we spit at others, yet it winds up poisoning us. This is clear in the moment of a particularly venomous remark when our face flushes, our heart rate jumps, we clench our jaws, and feel ready to ignite. It's not so much that emotions themselves are toxic, but that when we avoid their expression, they tend to come out anyway in convoluted, indirect, and exaggerated ways.

Let's say you hurt my feelings by inviting our friend Peggy to a concert instead of me. I say nada, I stew, and I become resentful. But I don't want you to know that. Frankly, I don't want to know you have the power to hurt me, either. So, I wind up forgetting, if you will, how angry I am. I also "forget" to invite you to my party, an acting-out measure that sends a message, yet still seems innocent enough to me. You're more willing to feel your feelings and you let our friends and I know you think I'm a dick for not including you. It's the emotions we're less aware of that often cause the most harm, the most toxic of which are those driven by righteousness and self-sufficiency. Both states make it hard to see our part in relationship problems.

Often without realizing it, dicks spend immense time and energy gathering evidence against others. We're so convinced they're wrong and we're right that when we wield our indignation, it actually feels like we're retaliating against an attack. Then we invest, sometimes pathologically, in constructing powerful rationalizations of how we were wronged and must now do something about it. Increasingly, we protect ourselves from what we want and need, inadvertently isolating ourselves. Painfully ensconced in a delusional self-sufficiency, we need no one because no one is good enough, or non-dickish enough, to meet our needs.

This is how the dick feels, but it's not how the dick acts. Instead, embracing the victim role, dicks corner those few remaining allies who can tolerate their behavior. They deliver criticism and blame, the message being *I'm hurt, someone caused it, and that must be you.* Taking out this supposedly justified anger on the people the dick is convinced caused it can become an obsessive pursuit. Anxiety and hurt evolve into compulsive activities as they bypass awareness altogether.

It's worth noting, though, that these behaviors may not be as overt as a direct onslaught of criticism and blame. Let's go back to the concert story. Why was it so hard to let our friend know that they hurt us by inviting Peggy instead of us? We all need some kind of evidence, usually from our childhood development, that it's safe to express uncomfortable feelings. Sadly, many in our society are taught *not to let 'em see you sweat.* We withhold how we really feel because:

1. It's not cool to look like a "wimp," or whatever

2. If people see the "real us" and reject it (as opposed to the persona we generally present), the rejection will crush us

3. And they'll know they can hurt us

The dick already believes people are going to hurt them. So, why hand over the ammunition to do so? In the last example, our hurt feelings and resentment were acted out as "forgetting" to invite you to our party. The rationale we came to was that we didn't want you to know you had the power to hurt us, which is to say that you mattered to us. Instead, our behavior told you.

Behavior is the language of the dick. It tells a story of hurt, fear, and anxiety that no one literally *hears* because the message is rendered indecipherable by bad behavior. Whether or not we can directly identify the cause of our pain, we're pissed, and we're going to take it out on someone. The anger is a secondary, protective reaction to our more vulnerable emotions of pain and fear.

As I've said, adversarial relationships often feel to dicks like righteous superiority, which come across as the stereotypical one-upmanship of a narcissist. However, a dick can be driven by an internal conflict between their need to be cared for and a compulsion to take care of others. This results in the dreaded sense that wrongs need to be righted, often at great personal and interpersonal expense.

Resentment over having to do this heavy lifting is a gift that keeps on giving. Not only do we feel burdened by the resentment itself, it clouds our vision so we see more people as enemies trying to pull a fast one on us. A dick is a resentment machine: induced toward bitter feelings and grudges that lead to pettiness and revenge. And what is resentment without obsession? Bitterness, jealousy, and the like all become emotional toxins when unaddressed. I mean, is there a resentful fantasy that doesn't lead to ruin if followed through on? Go ahead. Traverse that path and see what happens.

Eventually, as dicks, we use obsessively driven actions to avoid feelings of any kind and get caught up in patterns that help us avoid conscious awareness of emotional discomfort. This is a very limiting way to exist. Life without awareness of emotion can feel colorless, gray, and depressing. Actions fueled by the dissociated emotion still resemble that underlying emotion—we just lose access to information that might help us knock it off. Like: *Ugh, that was ugly, I shouldn't have been such a dick.*

You're entitled to take credit for what *works* in your relationship as well as responsibility for what's wrong. Generally speaking, though, proving that you're right is an isolating state. The other person is identified as wrong, and anyone consistently made to feel wrong will respond to their accuser as a dick eventually.

The Danger of Being Right

If *not* being a dick is truly your goal then the need to be right is your worst enemy. There is much to the question, "Would you rather be right or be happy?" (My wife's response to that question is, "Both.")

But if always being right resembles dickery, why would anyone crave that not-so-bright-and-shiny position? My years of clinical practice suggest that being right allows us to believe our indignation is justified. In this way, we rationalize all kinds of poor treatment of others without realizing we're using people as receptacles for what we cannot stand in ourselves.

Here's the kicker: being proven right doesn't make things *better*. It may just make them worse. People who know you're right may be unwilling to listen to you, follow instructions, or do what they're told simply to spite your poor behavior. The world is full of anti-authoritarian types just looking for a jerk to push back against, *especially* when that jerk is right!

Being strictly right or wrong are extreme positions, anyway. They create enmity between the world and ourselves. That said, we're not looking to suddenly flip our compass. A sense of safety between us and the world in which it feels okay to give up the equivocation is what's needed. This will allow us to accept what others have to say as merely a different point of view that we've protected ourselves from hearing. Sustaining a dangerous world that deserves our tough treatment has to stop.

We're not teachable when we're right all the time. The world has nothing to tell us, so all we do is recycle old impressions of how it works. This creates a mechanical, fixed set of routines between us and our environment. The definition of insanity is to "do the same thing over and over again while expecting different results." Dicks repeat their bad behavior and continually receive the same disappointing results. This confirms, to them, that the world is hostile. So, what to do then if repeating the "same thing" over and over again, complete with the "same results," no matter how upsetting and painful, is all we can do to protect ourselves from a world that feels overwhelming? Changing dickish behavior often requires that we go through a period of "insanity"— defined as unsoundness of mind—as we break out of old routines that were adopted to survive in difficult times.

Tim Against the World

My client Tim seemed like a mild-mannered social worker when he came to see me. He'd been having problems with Kelly, his most recent girlfriend, he said. I didn't understand the extent of their issues until later, though, when he abashedly shared his latest "airing our dirty laundry" incident.

"I really did it this time," Tim told me. "I ranted about a 'friend' on my blog, believing what I posted was vague enough that my girlfriend wouldn't recognize I was bitching about her. But Kelly knew who I was referring to, and it shocked her that I could get so angry. She'd never seen that side of me. Now she won't talk to me at all, and if I've ruined this relationship like I did all the others, I don't know what I'll do."

Since he expressed a strong willingness to work with me to try to save his relationship, I asked Tim to outline his life story, and some parts of the narrative really surprised me.

"My parents were children of the '60s, so their message was all peace, love, and understanding. Yet I saw their life as being more about self-involvement, absence, and neglect. As an '80s kid, my cultural mantra was the punk rock battle cry 'F— you!' I lived that motto perfectly. I had a rowdy band, blue Mohawk, the whole nine yards. Now, even though the leather pants and the rest of that scene is behind me, I have a strong impulse to defy everyone. Sometimes I feel like a walking middle finger held straight up in the air. I vent my anger at the people closest to me, like Kelly, and every girl I dated before her. Every time I'm in a relationship for longer than four months it feels like my very survival is at stake. Eventually, the person I'm dating can't take it."

I could tell Tim was struggling. We explored how the "punk" persona, which his family took as an affront, was an effort to be the family scapegoat. Therapists call this the *identified patient*. It's a person who acts out in ways that call attention to him or herself to distract from a serious problem. The identified patient essentially takes one for the team, and in so doing alienates the rest of the family, embracing the role of the black sheep. Though being a dick and the identified patient concept are not *exactly* the same, they serve a similar function. Both help distract others from an acute or chronic crisis and dissociate awareness of anxiety. For Tim, the first step in learning to act less like a dick was to see where his anxiety came from.

Tim said his parents struggled while he was in high school, which made sense. His "F— you" attitude was a perfect diversion from his family crisis. Like the proverbial scapegoat, Tim took the sins of his parents upon himself and took on the world as a dick. Even when he was no longer "so punk," he found subtle ways to piss people off.

There may be no better way to sustain in a psychologically defensive routine than through anger and rebellion. Tim acted like a dick in high school, taking on the persona of a punk and separating himself from the rest of his family, to manage the pain of his parents' battles, but his rebellion only maintained his experience of the conflict. He internalized the family's trouble to distract everyone from the real problem. But the fallout left him looking and feeling like a dick.

Tim took this behavior with him into adulthood, using it in every subsequent relationship. The only way he knew how to avoid being a dick was to avoid relationships entirely or sabotage them quickly. As he grew older, this mode of severe detachment from emotional experience became a coping mechanism that protected him, the would-be rebel, from recognizing that he actually felt highly invested in, and at risk of being banished from, whatever it was he believed he was fighting against. Safety, security, trust, acceptance—all that he defended against deep down he craved. Now, Tim's dickish persona operates as a protective measure against people like Kelly, whose affections threaten to evolve into another important emotional bond that eventually goes away.

Tim realized that being a dick had blocked him from developing lasting relationships. The repercussions were clear. He just didn't know how to correct the situation.

Tim needed to do self-inventory and make amends with his girlfriend. After we worked together for a few months, he told me, "Things are slowly getting better. I've not quite learned how not to screw up, but I'm learning how to mend things when I do."

If Tim can learn this lesson, so can you. Being a dick has likely thrown you into a negative social dynamic in which you act out unresolved conflicts, like Tim did for years after his family crisis. The anger fueling our bad behavior is purely reactive—not thought out, or representative of our whole range of feelings. And usually that reaction is to a perceived threat, as in *possible* harm, or to the vulnerability triggered when we're hurt or scared.

Again, dickishness is akin to brandishing a weapon, and makes us targets for offensive attacks and defensive withdrawal away from relationships. In the end, dominating, tyrannizing, and over-managing other people is self-defeating, as that aggressive way of relating triggers counterattacks that can become so acute, it appears as though the world is targeting us.

Putting Our Weapons Down

There will be times when we lay our weapons down, and there will be times when they drop unintentionally. Such was the case with my client Liam when he fell into a depression. Both his mother and maternal grandmother had been depressed during his childhood, so the condition ran in the family, but it still came as a surprise when it hit him in his early thirties.

"I was always the motivator in my family," Liam said. "Mr. Mom, they called me. I was the unofficial activities director and the primary breadwinner as well."

In response to his mother's depression, Liam picked up the slack. But he also looked for slack where there really wasn't any in order to justify his frequent complaints about doing others' work.

Liam tended not to act with modesty in his supportive endeavors, and by the time he was an adult, he often rubbed it in, pointing out to others, such as his wife and kids, that they couldn't pull their own weight. When he "helped" them (he honestly felt like he was being nice), he emphasized "how to do things *right*."

Hard to imagine this came off well, but somehow the formula allowed the family to function. In Liam's opinion, his role as over-manager was all that kept them afloat. Thus, his biggest concern when the depression hit was how his wife Jeanne would handle the family without his full presence.

Taking one look at Liam, it was clear something was off; he dreaded admitting to his wife that he wasn't, as he put it, "operating at top speed."

Liam's management did indeed slip. Yet as it did, Jeanne and the kids proved more than able. No one said a word. For a time, Liam's mood and mental state did not improve. It became for him a kind of elephant in the room.

"No one noticed it, or at least no one said anything about it," Liam recalled. "By the time I felt ready to tell Jeanne I was depressed, I'd convinced myself she wouldn't accept me in this state. To prepare for my announcement, I asked if she noticed anything different over the past month. She said, 'Of course, Liam. I've been concerned about you. I was driving myself nuts at first trying to figure out how to help, or what to say even. I was stumped. But then as time went by my concern turned into relief. It was the first time since we'd met that you weren't all over me, telling me what to do, how to do it, criticizing me, making me feel like a child.'"

Liam was still having trouble processing that this had happened. "I was shocked," he admitted. "Had I really been such a bully?"

Never one to let a crisis go to waste, Liam gained valuable insight into what it's like to live under the duress of his constant over-management. His conversation with Jeanne served as a *window of opportunity* for them to commit to a more equal partnership.

"I'm recovering from the depression now," said Liam. "And Jeanne and I and the whole family, it seems, are recovering from being estranged from each other in the very same home."

Brandishing the weapon of helpfulness (I sometimes refer to it as *helpaholism*), sharpened with unrealistic expectations and resentment, made Liam difficult to tolerate, which he took as further reason to withdraw into defensiveness. Dominating other people triggers counterattacks that can become so common, they evolve into the norm. This goes to show how entrenched the pattern can become in relationships, families, and workplace dynamics, until the dick steps back and realizes that he or she isn't being so helpful at all.

"It's odd to be so grateful for bottoming out so hard," concluded Liam.

You Can't Outthink Your Feelings

At a minimum, our feelings motivate us to get our basic needs met. Beyond that, emotions give us up-to-date and comprehensive information about what's happening in the world around us. Most of this goes on unconsciously, so it can be hard if not impossible to know when we're guarding ourselves from overwhelming emotions. Anxiety, *the overestimation of danger and the underestimation of our ability to cope*, is especially common, but often hard to acknowledge, because our mind is geared to suppress our awareness of experiences that threaten our sense of self or our ability to function. As with all emotions, though, anxiety is valuable as a kind of roadmap for living. Emotions are the interface we use to understand people, and living without an intact emotional life can have devastating effects on us and those around us.[18]

Our feelings demand expression. Quite simply, we cannot think ourselves out of the human condition. When feelings are denied they find creative and even bizarre ways out into the open. Even when we implement dissociation, the most complex psychological defense technique for eradicating awareness of anxiety, our feelings tend to reveal themselves to others by our actions and inactions, if not to ourselves. As an emotional experience, however, dissociation is less like fear, which it sidelines, and more like an itch you cannot scratch. While the purpose of dissociation is to not be present, an uncanny sensation persists. Somehow things just aren't right. In a dissociated state, we may go so far as to invent new personalities that become discrete alter egos for troubling moods, histories, and other identifying features. The great interpersonal psychiatrist Harry Stack Sullivan referred to the extreme state of experiencing oneself while by being psychologically dissociated as "not-me" states. Underlying feelings of terror are so extreme we can hardly acknowledge them—or know ourselves while we're in them. In "not-me" states, dissociation unintentionally protects us from the full range of emotional experiences I know as "me."[19] Dissociation is a tremendously hard place to reach, be it through attempts to get in touch with ourselves or when others try to connect with us. But with determination and support, recognizing dissociative patterns can lead us back to a basic level of reachability.

Sometimes we can break out of dissociation by surprise. Years of living in "not-me" states loosen, and we lower our defenses and let people reach us in ways that shock us. Such was the case with my client Ava. During a session, she relayed some fears about her relationship with a younger man. "Do you think when he finally throws me out, I'll be alone for the rest of my life?" she asked.

"No," I said. "There are plenty more wounded birds out there who need your help."

Consternation and anger passed over Ava's face. Tears fell. "I've never been with a man who wasn't insane and abusive."

"Never?" I asked.

"Well, my first husband was nice. He loved me and he never hurt me. He wanted us to have children. Be happy. He lived to serve me."

"What happened?"

"I couldn't take it! That sort of relationship is alien to me. I ruined it. I could not convince myself that my mixed feelings about him were normal and it drove me crazy. I was the insane one in that marriage. *I* acted abusive toward *him.*"

When Ava feels threatened, she shuts down, checks out, and becomes the dick. This exemplifies the truism that *you cannot outthink your feelings.* Those emotions that make you uncomfortable, stressed-out, fearful, angry, or any other emotional state you find unacceptable are especially likely to show up in your behavior. Not only that, dissociated feelings are likely to influence your patterns of interaction with the people you're closest to.

I'd known Ava long enough to know her feelings are tuned to protect her heart, and that her behavior toward men bulwarked her against each new prospect. The pattern had played out her entire romantic life. Of course, this doesn't mean she will be alone forever. But it does suggest that to some extent being rejected and abandoned is her motive. Being proven unlovable once again ends the madness associated with hoping that the man she likes actually cares about her. With this conflicted sense of desire and insecurity, she can only feel *safe* in two types of situations:

1. A relationship with a dick

2. A relationship with a man whose kindness frightens her, triggering her to be the dick

In either case, she doesn't have to accept herself or someone else—as is. Dissociation causes Ava to not be present, but there's still the uncanny sense that something is off. In a dissociated state, Ava became the dick—rejecting those who cared for her, and in so doing, she reenacted her worst fear.

When pushed to the extreme, these mighty efforts to protect ourselves from the world backfire and leave us sad, lonely, and isolated, yet at the same time safe from being aware that we're hurt. In our heads, however, we still bring others into this self-imposed isolation. Anger, pain, and resentment persist, and through these emotions we stay connected, internally, to those who've hurt us. New relationships drum up those old displaced feelings, and without intending to, we react by pushing people away.

Ava had a very hard time connecting the dots between her early history of hurt and disappointment at the hands of parents who lived by the motto, "children are to be seen and not heard," to her conflicted relationships with men. But when she did, torrents of anger, covering up decades of dissociated hurt, came blasting into our sessions. Initially, these were directed at me. Then as Ava processed and worked through the hurt, which she had experienced as "mixed feelings," she was able to accept being seen and heard by the man she was involved with.

Shut Down

Freud initially called depression "anger turned inward," as in hostility that sees the self as its primary target. Depression's job is to destroy and shut the self down. Another term for this is *introjected rage*. In his essay "Mourning and Melancholia," Freud suggested that depression is unconscious mourning.[20] According to this theory, the unconscious is like a vault for early life grief where we store pain from major losses, such as the death of a loved one. At first this leads to outward anger, then the anger converts to guilt, and is finally turned inward.

Although depression is a debilitating condition, severe dicks often see it as a vacation from having to feel.[21] And when it's actual *DSM-5*-level depression, we don't so much outthink our feelings as become consumed by them until we totally shut down.

So it went with another client of mine, Ethan. At age forty-two, he fell in love for the first time. Obviously, that was a good thing. Trouble came when he acted out in standoffish ways that, in his words, "threatened to kill the relationship." Through an increasingly apathetic attitude and withholding behavior, Ethan more or less told his "love," Nora, to "go screw off." In short, he'd been a dick.

As we worked together, Ethan realized he had repeated a terrifying behavioral pattern that developed when he was seven, when his father began to exhibit bizarre behavior, mostly of a suspicious and increasingly paranoid nature. Ethan's father was a prominent psychiatrist tormented by persecutory thoughts regarding professional rivals. He'd say things like, "Other doctors have our house under surveillance." His behavior embarrassed Ethan. He hated his dad for it, but he also hated people who lacked compassion for his father. Ethan believed his dad's paranoia was a cry for help. Both Ethan and his dad felt ashamed, and despite strong concerns from his mother, Ethan spent as much time as he could with his father. He developed a powerful sense of obligation to protect his dad from cruel treatment, especially from his mother and their extended family, believing what they were saying and doing was unfair.

Ultimately, Ethan failed to fix his dad. In fact, the opposite occurred; Ethan's father believed Ethan was partly responsible for his condition. During this time, Ethan began to emulate his father's chronic anxiety and social phobia. It haunted him for years, but was hard for Ethan to understand as an adult. He acted out his anxiety in a performance meant to distract from the catastrophe that was his childhood inability to care for his father. Ethan grew up to become a comedian prone to biting sarcasm (go figure) that he mostly directed at people in the profession his father thought was "after him" when Ethan was a boy (that would be, ahem, his shrink). At the core of Ethan's dark, often-hurtful routine was an animosity to anyone who came near him. It was only as a comedian that he could interact with people. He lived in fear that anyone who got close to him in normal life would see the pain, fear, and anxiety behind his humor.

Nora loved Ethan's comedy. It's what first attracted her to him. But then she realized it wasn't just a routine. By then she cared about him and was willing to give him a chance if he'd just deal with whatever was causing him to push her away. Ethan took her up on the challenge and entered therapy for the umpteenth time. This time, with me.

In the beginning, he constantly complained he was "not getting better." All he really wanted to do was get back with his girlfriend and "feel nothing at all," he said. He just wanted the pain to stop so he could move on and "be a good boyfriend for Nora." But until he really began to address, work through, and express his deep fear of allowing himself to care for and be cared for by another person, he continued to act in ways that upset and pushed people away. The routine was working exactly the way it was designed to: it kept people away. But now he was in a terrible conundrum because it had driven a wedge between him and a person who had somehow gotten past his defenses and begun to matter. Nora was challenging Ethan with the possibility that someone could love him even though he was "not well"—anxious, scared, standoffish, dickish—as his father had been before everyone but Ethan deserted him.

Ethan became increasingly aware of how angry he was at everyone who abandoned his father—and abandoned Ethan in his effort to care for his dad. Ethan played out this dynamic with me, often becoming enraged because he felt like I was withholding some therapeutic secret that would cure him. He blasted me. And in my own sense of failure, I was able to put myself in his shoes to get a visceral look at the deep sense of failure Ethan carried inside him. Being the single, lonely, dark, and sarcastic comedian, he had tried for years to act in accordance with his shame, a state of humiliation that he shared with me in his actions more so than his words. It was also clear—and hopeful—that he was finally fed up with this hopeless state. Instead of seeking clever ways to tell everyone who threatened to care about him to screw off (including his "bad therapist") he was getting in touch with his underlying pain.

If we can't stand our anger, (and Ethan was unable to tolerate his own rage and hatred for years on end) we shut down. The world offers many ways to distance and distract ourselves from what we feel, but that can only go so far. We wind up acting out those feelings, even when doing so leads to self-destructive habits, or toxic relationship patterns. When all our scorecards read zero, it creates the absolute need to escape to a state in which everything is leveled, everything is predictable, and every encounter feels like every other experience. That state is depression.

Depression, dissociation, dickery—whatever you want to call it—created and sustained Ethan's isolation. But in therapy he could allow himself to express the underlying hurt and fear that his younger self turned off when he couldn't help his father. Through this work, those issues became easier to deal with in his relationship with Nora, who did stick around. She saw something in Ethan he had a hard time seeing in himself—that his dickery was just an expression of pain and a call for help. Expressing and sharing his pain in a calm, sincere way wound up being much easier for both of them to live with than the sarcasm, the raging, and the emotional shutting down. By putting the weapon of dickery down, Ethan broke free from years of isolating behavior.

Attachment Style and Being a Dick

While high-functioning people may appear emotionally secure, those with an adversarial relationship to the world lock down their emotions to conceal what clinicians call an *insecure attachment style*. This limits how well they access experience, so the way they perceive and relate within relationships is stunted. Research on attachment style finds a connection between limited dynamics in adults and how they related to their primary caregivers as children.[22] The greater your demand for intimacy as an adult, the more crucial your attachment style becomes.

Attachment styles are generally classified as either secure or insecure (i.e., avoidant or anxious) depending on the quality of your childhood caregiving, innate factors with which you're born, and the fit between you and your caregiver's attachment styles.[23] People with secure attachment styles typically remain grounded during emotional disruptions, and even during severe life crises. They experience emotions and go through life-upsets without becoming profoundly disturbed and can return to equilibrium relatively quickly. By contrast, a person with an insecure attachment style experiences the normal ups and downs of life as so intense, they can only function in relationships by avoiding anything that might trigger anxiety. This may mean avoiding or dismissing interpersonal connections altogether.

Since we can't pick and choose which emotions we keep at a distance, blocking distressing emotions interferes with the ability to tolerate *any* type of frank emotional experience, even positive feelings like empathy, joy, and love. The behavior can snowball rapidly. If an adult who avoids intimacy gets involved with someone with an anxious attachment style, the avoidant person will increasingly retreat from the other's advances, evoking more worried pursuit. This sets up a cycle that builds to a dramatic resolution—one usually unpleasant. Similarly, relationships may slowly deaden when two avoidant people leave dissatisfactions unresolved for long periods of time, diminishing their ability to resolve them. Disappointment gives way to chronic feelings of deprivation, resentment, and suppressed contempt. If communication doesn't improve, sadness and grief are added to the mix. Someone's bound to become a dick; one encroaches while the other estranges.

Is that it then? People born into family situations that resulted in insecure attachment styles are doomed to be reactive rather than responsive in relationships? Of course not. That's not what attachment theory nor my own clinical practice indicate. An "earned secure attachment,"[24] the style that allows us to break down habitual roles and routines, is entirely attainable if we work to clear away our confused ideas about relationships, explore our feelings and needs, and hit pause when tempted to act like dicks.

Managing to express complex emotions in relationships is daunting at first. It often triggers anxiety and even makes dickish reactions seem reasonable. But just being *open* to new ways of relating with others can create a new outcome between you and the world.

Sidebar: A Study in Not Being a Dick

Incidentally, I'm finding that even as I write a book about not being a dick, it's hard not to be a dick in the process. Whether describing my own incidents and patterns, those I hear about in my work and personal life (anonymously, of course), or those I witness in public, I'm tempted to write like a dick about such behavior. The process is *isomorphic*, which is when what you're talking or writing about plays out in the process of describing it.

Once, a former client of mine, who during years of therapy complained bitterly about her circumstances yet resisted any action that might lead to actual change, wrote me an email saying that although I'd "screwed" her, she needed to come back to therapy.

Wait, *what*?

It reminded me of a joke about the couple at a diner where the man says, "The food here is awful," and the woman replies, "Yeah, and they don't give you nearly enough of it."

She slipped in something that hurt my feelings, triggered a defensive reaction in me, and then became an example of how hard it is to *not be a dick* when receiving what feels like a sucker punch. Yes, she wanted to come back, and P.S., her note read, "I do hope you're more helpful this time."

Addressing our knee-jerk sensitivities to being hurt is the same challenge as accepting people who push our buttons. How do we balance being reactive to their harm (acting like dicks with no chance of respite or reparation) and being mindful enough to respond in ways that leave room for understanding? The real challenge in relationships is not in identifying who's a dick, it's in limiting our own dickery so we stop the cycle.

When my client returned to therapy, I flashed a genuine smile. And my challenge in writing this book is not simply to resist the compulsion to isomorph the hell out of this process with my own dickery, but also to acknowledge that this is as much my struggle as yours, and to ask that you join me in developing a process to deal with anger and pain in ways that are ours.

EXERCISE: EXPLORING YOUR HISTORICAL PATTERN OF DICKERY AND ITS INFLUENCE

To get a handle on how being a dick materializes in your relationships, look at some of the patterns and behaviors you've experienced—and likely learned—from your family history that were negative or hurtful.

Relationship patterns and behaviors modeled for me	The family members involved in these patterns and behaviors	The impact of these patterns and behaviors on me now
Example A: I saw my parents treat each other terribly, but no matter how bad it got they said I was "lucky" to have two parents, or any parents at all.	My parents	I overlook what would otherwise seem like intolerable behavior from my friends and romantic partners.
Example B: My dad complained bitterly about my mom to my siblings and I. Yet he never addressed how he felt directly to her.	My dad	I learned not to tell anyone what I think or feel about their behavior. This means I stew with resentment that only helps me devalue my partners.

CONTINUED ON NEXT PAGE

Relationship patterns and behaviors modeled for me	The family members involved in these patterns and behaviors	The impact of these patterns and behaviors on me now

Now, using the examples A and B for reference, describe two or three of your own relationship patterns. These behaviors are what I call your "enactment" with the world. After that, consider the following:

- What does the way you relate to others suggest about how you use attitudes and actions to protect yourself?

- How rigid are these relational patterns? And the attitudes and actions that go with them?

- Is it possible that these enactments—your default ways of relating to others—set you up to be hurt?

- Given what you've learned so far, how malleable might these interaction patterns be?

- Who taught you to protect yourself in these dickish ways?

- Might the transformation you seek come from changing your relationship dynamic? What might that look like?

The Consequences of Dickish Behavior

Being a dick leaves an indelible mark on those we hurt. And like debt, it accrues interest paid through attacks on you. If you've been a dick, you can bet the farm you've caused all kinds of resentment in others. They'll be gunning for you, perhaps for a long time to come. So isn't it imperative to know how your behavior causes anger and pain in others? The patterns we exhibit allow our feelings to bypass our awareness since they're uncomfortable and scary. But these behaviors also constitute examples of the "self" that put us in a position to receive further hurt.

The Nut Punch of the Mama Bear

How does the mind protect itself when our internal voice evolves into an enemy within? We build a psychological defense system. One example of that is acting like a dick. A more productive method is to accept people from far, far away. That means that when people prove themselves to be unkind or hurtful, it's best to avoid them. Not being a dick does not require us to accept or tolerate mistreatment from other people.

"You know, I admire the way you did nothing when those girls teased your daughter," a once-seemingly-friendly mother said to a dad at a dance class.

Can we have an adversarial relationship with our environment? In other words, can we be so concerned about being mistreated, and so trigger-happy with our reactions, that unbeknownst to ourselves we preemptively mistreat others? Yes, and it often looks like this: righteous superiority and attempts at one-upmanship.

"I'm not a Tiger Mom. I'm a Mama Bear," continued the no-longer-friendly mom. "Unlike you, I couldn't stand pat and watch my kid go through that."

Internally, adversarial relationships with one's environment can be driven by unresolved conflicts between a need to be cared for and a compulsion to take care of others. The result is a dreaded sense that wrongs need to be *righted*, and often at great personal expense the dick is compelled to right them.

"Tiger Mom" is a strict disciplinarian parenting concept popularized by Amy Chua in her book, *Battle Hymn of the Tiger Mother*.[25]

Mama Bear missed the part when Chua stated that her narration was meant to be ironic and self-mocking.[26] In response to a backlash against the book's severe advice, Chau also said "in retrospect, these coaching suggestions seem a bit extreme." Nonetheless, many people have read *The Battle Hymn of the Tiger Mother* as gospel. *A Nation of Wimps* author and *Psychology Today* editor at large Hara Estroff Marano marshaled evidence supporting Chua's approach.[27] And Mama Bear seemed to want to take the animal instinct thing to a new level. She could not pause long enough to assess the situation and see that the dad was juggling two children unexpectedly because his wife was ill and that the screaming three-year-old actually feigned her tears, gleefully enjoying, as she was, a kind of teasing game with her older sister and friends.

Urban Dictionary defines Mama Bear as "a mom who can be cuddly and lovable but also has a ferocious side when it's necessary to protect her cubs." In this case, being a Mama Bear also appeared to be a justification to act like a dick to people who, in her estimation, were not parenting right. When we act self-protective and adversarial in our world, we play out a precarious dynamic one not-quite-right individual at a time. Out to set things straight, we repeat over and over: *you're wrong*. And of course the world reacts. Recall that Alcoholics Anonymous quote about how we step on the toes of our fellows and they retaliate. The anxiety-reducing aspect of holier-than-thou dickery blocks our awareness of the fact that few people want to be helped in a condescending way.

Although Mama Bear's remarks felt like a surprise nut punch, the dad didn't respond directly. Instead, he committed to protecting himself from what he recognized as toxic, mean, petty self-righteousness. From that point on, he would no longer engage with Mama Bear. And while she had little comprehension of the dick role she was in, being shut out by a social acquaintance was not at all alien to her.

A psychoanalyst might ask: Was it a relationship she was still in with the world of her upbringing? Does being a Mama Bear somehow compensate for dreams that didn't come true? Is it possible the dad inadvertently stepped on the battlefield of her internal conflicts and received a nut punch she intended for those who hurt her earlier?

At the end of the dance class the dad broke his commitment not to engage the Mama Bear. "Go fur yourself," he told her as he left.

To be a dick is to walk through life with a "kick me" sign on. It's an invitation for near constant conflict and revises the old saying "the best defense is a good offense," because your defensiveness is so offensive it sets you up for a lifetime of retaliation. (The appropriate phrase here is *f— me!*).

It's time to settle up on the debt we owe those who believe justice will only be served when we've been hurt back. In the next chapter, we'll determine what kind of relationship we might have with our own dickery.

CHAPTER THREE

Dickery Is a Mood-Altering Drug

Looking for an attitude adjuster? Want to feel differently about yourself, the world, and your place in it? Go ahead and be a dick. It's amazing, instantaneous in fact, how quickly the world changes. Maybe that's why some of us seek out toxic situations; we can shore ourselves up against the world and our most vulnerable feelings about ourselves and others.

Throughout the first ten years of their relationship, Elise had a spring-loaded criticism ready any time her wife Pat brought up things that made her uncomfortable, such as their feelings for one another. Over the long haul Elise felt like a dick about this, so she did something about it. She tried to increase her awareness of what set her dickery off, account for it, and make amends as soon as possible. Like a mood-altering substance, this changed how she handled anxiety in relationships.

Elise made significant progress, yet she noticed that whenever she made amends, Pat would throw gas on the fire of their conflict. Instead of accepting the apology, Pat would run down a list of unaccounted-for criticisms—previous incidents committed by Elise. Pat became the dick in the relationship.

Something hard to see when we're caught in the cycle of being dicks to each other is that this behavior serves many purposes. The dick provides a scapegoat for problems in the relationship. As I mentioned in Chapter Two, family therapists call this role the "identified patient." It allows people in dysfunctional relationships to avoid the hard work of identifying everyone who contributed to the problem at hand, and similar problems in the past. Doing so changes the emotional atmosphere in a relationship. Taking on the scapegoat role as a dick charges the environment with an intensity that makes us a lightning rod that attracts and absorbs the bad feelings around and within us. If one person in a relationship habitually inhabits that scapegoat-dick role, the others may come to rely on, expect, and brace for it. It can put all parties in a chronic state of vigilance. Around the scapegoat-dick everyone is on guard. The role can make us feel powerful and righteous, as well as a bit manic, which is not something everyone involved will easily let go of.

"Is there a reason you won't simply accept my apology?" Elise finally asked. She didn't get the answer she expected.

"No reason I'm aware of," Pat admitted.

I can't tell you how many times I've seen this situation. As soon as one person puts down their dickery, ceasing the attacks on their partner, the person who cannot stop counterattacking, or refuses to accept the apology, stands out as the dick. It's a problem that embarrasses the stubborn arguer and makes their once valid attitude seem unsubstantiated. I've also seen occasions in which, after one person stops being a dick, the other person so thoroughly embraces the "bad guy" role, they feel convinced they were the dick all along.

When one person consistently acts like a dick in a relationship, it results in what feels like a predictable emotional environment. Others know what to expect from that person, so when they stop being the dick, there may be some initial resistance. Without that person as the scapegoat for all the problems in the relationship, ongoing troubles suddenly belong to *both* individuals.

You know the word SNAFU? Most people think it means a mistake. But it's actually a World War II era acronym for "Situation Normal: All F—ked Up." When the normalcy of a relationship is one of dickish behavior, both parties have apparently grown comfortable with it. By taking responsibility for her behavior and mending her ways, Elise undid the SNAFU, creating abnormality in their relationship by threatening to unf—k it up.

Being a dick in a relationship—be it platonic or romantic—lets everyone else off the hook for less apparent ways they too are dicks.

In all matters involving dickery, it takes two to tango. But there is also a third entity: the relationship itself. So the dynamic is me (the scapegoated overt dick), you (the passive one), and us (one big SNAFU). When you go on the offensive against a person who halted their dickish behavior, that's like setting a trap for someone else to step into. If the attacked person refuses to counterattack, the attacker tends then to believe the trap was set for them. They've stepped right into it (Ssssnnaap!), and look like the dick.

Elise responded to Pat's sudden willingness to assess her own behavior by saying, "Who knew it would be so hard to get you to accept my apologies?"

"Who knew your apology would turn into a request that I look at my role in our problems," Pat countered quietly.

A Relationship with Being a Dick

What kind of relationship might we have with dickery? Some spiritual systems and psychological theories suggest we have trouble letting go of what we term *character defects*—personality traits that result in us being dicks—and perhaps that's because they have their benefits. Bill Wilson, cofounder of Alcoholics Anonymous, famously said, "We still loved some of [our character defects] too much." For example, we may believe we're always innocent of wrongdoing and everyone else is at fault—a costly attitude to drop.

This idea of loving character defects too much is an opening. We can begin to view our dickish behavior as something we have a relationship with. Once we acknowledge what those "gains" are, we can do something about them. We can see what we're really giving up.

Many of us have love/hate relationships with our character defects and appear ambivalent or conflicted when it comes to halting our dickery. Now at first pass this ambivalence seems like a middle ground, but often we use it as an excuse to hold onto a behavior we're not yet able to relinquish. Waiting until we feel *ready* to do something, by the way, is how we camouflage our resistance to actual change. Using ambivalence to rationalize doing nothing is in itself a decision. It suggests we're convinced we don't need a personal transformation *yet*. In truth, a defensive position against change tends to happen because transformation is frightening. If we relinquish these traits, who will we become?

For couples, ambivalence to change often teeters between a healthy independence and a fear of being swallowed whole by someone else's needs. And while ambivalence is not a character defect in itself, it often triggers our own and other's character defects.

Carrie and Emmet ran through a number of couples' therapists prior to landing on my couch. Emmet was in his late forties, Carrie in her late thirties, and while they had no plans to marry, the issue of commitment was burning between them. Evidently, when they met they agreed "marriage was just a piece of paper." Emmet took this as a rigidly shared value. But Carrie now experienced Emmet's resistance to marriage as an unwillingness to commit.

"I am and have been committed," Emmet barked. "This is a deal-breaker."

"Deal-breaker?" Carrie shouted. "The real deal-breaker, Emmet, is that you've been acting like a jerk! You get upset and stay out all night. You don't come home, or when you do you bombard me with threats and then shut me out completely."

Carrie and Emmet's rage was so intense it was hard to see what else was going on. It took time, but enlightening questions finally squeezed forth between the lines of their anger, pain, and fear.

It turned out this was the same issue that caused Emmet's last relationship to blow up. Emmet was onboard to tie the knot then, but he used the same dickish behavior to get out of what felt like "a trap." The threat was not marriage or commitment; it was his agony over whether his ambivalence could be overcome in a loving relationship. Rather than accepting and learning to live with his own ambivalence, his dickish reaction made the decision for him; he avoided the real question: *Am I lovable, or not?*

Emmet believed his and Carrie's initial agreement allowed him to sidestep the challenge. It was born of his conscious terror of being trapped, and he'd felt relieved to find a woman who saw marriage as an outdated institution. Because that was a premise of their relationship, Emmet and Carrie both overlooked the fact that the issue was not about formalizing their relationship, but rather Emmet's horrible behavior when a partner's needs and desires freaked him out. He grew up with abusive, neglectful parents. His ambivalence and dickishness helped him avoid the lovability question, which his caregivers had ostensibly answered in the way they mistreated him.

A couples' work mentor of mine once said, "One dynamic that never resolves in a long-term relationship is *in-out*"—another way of describing ambivalence. She explained that when we bring our mixed feelings, push-and-pull dynamics, hesitations, and conflicts between being emotionally *in or out* into intimate relationships, these feelings do not resolve, they flourish, shift, and transform our experience of each other and ourselves. It's this uncertainty, a kind of ambivalence, that makes long-term relationships so enlivening as we navigate the uncertainties of everyday life together. The work of long-term love, however, is not to force one side of ambivalence to override the other— say, "I want you" instead of "I don't." The mind and heart are places where contradictions don't necessarily cancel each other out. The real issue of long-term love day in and day out is whether or not we can accept each other and ourselves exactly as we are. When we're dicks, we don't address the deeper issues of acceptability; we accept or reject based solely on our behavior. The underlying issue of lovability is avoided.

Emmet and Carrie eventually discovered that Emmet's dickish behavior was meant to express unequivocally that Emmet was unworthy of love. His dickery tried to convey that his behavior was the problem, not his lack of self-worth. That way, the inevitable rejection would not be about *him*. Realizing this, and feeling Carrie's persistent love throughout their struggle, allowed Emmet to put his protective acting out down and instead allow himself to love and be loved—mixed feelings and all.

EXERCISE: WILLINGNESS TO LET GO
Not being a dick is not about depriving ourselves of needed defenses, but about learning to do things differently. This exercise will allow you to assess your willingness to replace your character defects with healthier practices.

Describe your dickish behavior as you experience it, and then consider a positive quality that could replace it:

Character defects I can live without	Behaviors and qualities I can work toward to replace this defect
Examples: Lying Passive aggressive behavior	Examples: Openness and honesty with my partner Being assertive about my wants and needs
1.	1.
2.	2.
3.	3.
4.	4.
5.	5.

When Walking on Fire

You would think walking on fire would charbroil your feet. The mind naturally deters us from such dangers, a great primal instinct. But in fact, rather than having your feet burn, small blisters form on your soles. These are called "fire kisses" and are thought to represent doubts that the firewalker could endure the impossible-seeming conditions.

Fire walking is not about mind over matter. It's about fearing something immensely and yet going ahead and doing it anyway.

If we buy into the notion that character is the sum total of one's psychological defenses, we can see character defects like fire kisses. They express doubt that we're okay the way we are. In many ways, character defects double as survival skills. We attack the world for perceived injustice, believing we're engaged in counterattacks; the injustice, though, is a lingering hurt we have to rectify before we can be at peace with ourselves and others.

Recognizing our character defects as defenses developed to protect us from a hostile world allows us to consider the possibility that we're no longer exposed to that toxic environment in which we were forged. Letting them go is about forming a different kind of relationship to the world. But it's not that easy to convince ourselves we'll survive without our defensiveness; it takes experimenting with that hypothesis and seeing for ourselves in significant relationships that the costs of being a dick far outweigh the rewards.

Whatever secondary gain we achieve by being a dick, such as being seen as tough, no-nonsense, or a straight shooter, the actual "benefit" is being sidelined from anything resembling intimate human contact. Many of us go to great lengths to sustain that kind of "safety," but its price is isolation. Being a dick is a fear-based stance, and those who live in that solitary confinement are avoiding the fire walks of life.

EXERCISE: BEING A DICK USED TO EXPRESS EMOTION

The following chart is meant to assess behaviors that block our awareness of anxiety, list people who apply this behavior, and collect its outcomes.

Dick Behavior	Who Used the Behavior and Why	Target of the Behavior	Impact of the Behavior
Example A: Gossiping about neighbors; comparing their family to ours.	Mother usually instigated, but the rest of us would join in. It distracted us from uncomfortable feelings— mostly insecurity and envy—we had for each other.	The whole family.	Devaluing our neighbors created a one-sided negative feeling that ended up distancing us from them.
Example B: Frequent drug use; family pretended to be unaware, leading to neglect.	My parents always used drugs "recre-ationally," but it got worse as my sister and I got older. She and I pretend-ed it was normal and everything was okay.	My sister, me, our friends, the whole neighborhood.	My sister and I suppressed our anxiety about our parents and ignored problems it created with friends, school, and neighbors.

Now, using the above samples as a reference, write down two or three examples of your own dickery, including the targets of your behavior, who modeled it for you, and what its impact has been.

Afterward, try to give that impact even more context:

- Can you see any familiarity between past and present behaviors?

- Do you recognize the way it affects people around you? What is it doing for you?

- What do you see as the secondary gain of such behavior? For instance, does it keep bothersome people away? Has it helped you end taxing romantic or platonic relationships?

- What does your dickery suggest about how you have used attitudes and actions to protect yourself?

- How rigid are the attitudes and actions that go with your dickery?

- Given what you've learned so far, how malleable might these interaction patterns be?

- Who taught you to protect yourself in these dickish ways?

- Might the transformation you seek come from changing the relationship dynamic between you and the world? What might that look like?

CHAPTER FOUR

Punching Bag

You know that emotions in and of themselves are not toxic. But when negative emotions aren't dealt with, they can bypass awareness and be acted out in behavior, or *enacted* as relationship patterns, in highly destructive ways. You might say our relationships with others reflect our past experience and ongoing understanding of ourselves vis-à-vis the world. This starts with our initial primary caretakers, and it's imperative to understand this dynamic.

Unresolved dickery leads to failed relationships, trouble at work, and emotional difficulties for which the source is often difficult to trace. Dickery balks at investigation. It manifests in a myriad of expressions that include deep-seated self-doubt, self-pity, and self-contempt. So, if we are to achieve anything like harmony, we might need a heads-up on what John and Julie Gottman, the world's premier relationship experts, call relationship killers *par excellence*. These also happen to be the ways that being a dick comes across to others:

1. **Criticism**, an attack on another's character or personality. Here are examples to note the difference between a complaint and criticism; *Complaint*: "There's no gas in the car and I'm annoyed you didn't fill it up like you said you would." *Criticism*: "You never remember anything! You're completely unreliable. I can't count on your word at all!"

2. **Contempt**, a behavior that communicates disgust, including but not limited to sneering, sarcasm, name-calling, eye rolling, mockery, mean humor, and condescension. Contempt is primarily delivered through nonverbal behaviors. It prevents

two people from reconciling, inevitably increases conflict, and is always disrespectful. The Gottmans' research shows that couples who display contempt for each other suffer more instances of illness and disease than respectful couples.

3. **Defensiveness**. These behaviors convey the message, "The problem isn't me. It's *you*." This implies that because your partner threw the first stone, they're responsible for the ensuing conflict. You avoid taking responsibility for your behavior by pointing to something they did prior to the complaint about you. You don't acknowledge the truth in what they say about your attitude and your behavior.

4. **Stonewalling**. In relationships where intense arguments break out and criticism and contempt lead to defensiveness, one partner eventually tunes out. This is stonewalling. The stonewaller acts as if he (the Gottmans' research indicates that 85 percent of stonewallers in marriages are husbands) couldn't care less what his partner says or does, and turns away from conflict *and* the relationship. Any form of disengagement is stonewalling.

These relationship killers are equally effective at excusing one's own bad behavior. We regularly use them against ourselves, believing things like resentment and revenge are defensive measures against others when in fact they hurt, stifle, and isolate us.

When we're hurt, we tend to be unable to leave the scene of the crime. Over and over again, through obsessions and compulsions that allow our emotions to slide right under the tripwire of consciousness, we return to our pain during interactions with the world, subjecting others to our messy bog of unresolved conflict.

When we're stressed out and feel out of control, our response can lead to actions that don't allow others to help remedy the situation. That's when we feel lonely, even though supportive people are right there with us. Instead of turning to them, we use our out-of-control feelings to justify protecting ourselves from them; after all, they're as likely to be responsible for the problem as for its solution. We act out like dicks.

A crisis is often a window into how our defenses come out, isolate us, and reinforce dissociation of what we want and need from others.

I have a client named Sam whose mother said repeatedly throughout his childhood that she loved him, but he had a difficult time believing it, and ultimately couldn't accept that she cared for him. Because Sam's father worked feverishly hard to make ends meet, his mother said she felt like a single mom. She had two other kids to take care of, and so the attention and direct care that she could offer didn't feel to Sam like enough. Intellectually, he understood his mother's dilemma, but deep down he felt withheld from and believed, "If she really loved me, she would find a way to be more present." He did all he could throughout his early years and adolescence to attract her attention in positive ways, but at some point he gave up and began punishing her and everyone else for his sense of helplessness.

Since Sam felt underappreciated when he tried to be a "good kid," he came to believe that nothing he did could result in a positive response. He turned to dickery, which felt like something he had more control over. You act like a dick and the world responds in consistent, albeit painful and negative, ways.[28]

Dickery, as I've said, often begins as a reaction to an early childhood environment (usually a parent) that feels out of control. That is why assessing our current responses to stress and feeling a lack of control is important. It helps us understand how our past comes out in our present relationships.

Catharsis and the Punching Bag[29]

The term catharsis was used by Aristotle to describe the emotional release experienced while watching Greek tragedies. It derived from *kathairein*, meaning *cleansing*. And we use catharsis as a rationale for venting our feelings; it's purifying for goodness' sake! Sigmund Freud helped push this idea into common practice. Mental wellness, he reasoned, could be achieved by purging impurities into the wastebasket that is a therapist.

Freud believed repressed fears and desires, unresolved conflicts, and unhealed wounds poison the psyche. The mind reacts by forming phobias and obsessions around these bits of mental flotsam, and what's needed is to rummage around in there, open up some vents, and let the pressure out. The hydraulic model of anger is just what it sounds like—anger builds up inside the mind until you let off some steam. If you don't, the boiler will burst. So, according to this theory, without catharsis you're likely to explode.

People in the helping professions have been attempting to dispel the effectiveness of this method for years. Harville Hendrix, for example, courageously revised his amazing 1988 book *Getting the Love You Want* in 2008 with a correction. The cathartic "getting it out" approach to conflict had been shown to backfire and be destructive in the long run.

According to David McRaney,[30] author of the blog *You Are Not So Smart*, which this section is based on, the notion that venting anger verbally is an effective way to reduce stress and avoid physically lashing out at a loved one is a misconception. In truth, venting increases aggressive behavior over time.

Hard to imagine, I know. Catharsis seems to make sense. And that meme about how "releasing sexual tension feels good," did so well.

McRaney says, "Throwing up when you are sick feels good. Finally getting to a restroom feels good." But using catharsis to justify hostility, despite its momentary relief, does not justify the consequence of living at odds with the world and with yourself.

Take Julie. Anyone could be her personal punching bag. Her anger toward the world was a telltale sign of unhappiness. She felt surprised, though— "shocked"—when her therapist said the point of their sessions was "not mere catharsis," and that no good would come from letting Julie treat her like a punching bag.

How well has it ever worked to treat people in your life like crap? Dr. Michael Bennett and his daughter Sarah Bennett, the renowned provocateurs of self-help, have this to say in their wildly popular book *F*ck Feelings*: "The sort of venting that goes on in couple's therapy is a lot like the venting of intestinal gas; it provides immediate relief for the venter, but soon poisons the air for everyone in the fallout zone."

To be fair, Julie had good reason to be angry. Much of what she wanted to address in therapy was pain that until then she had expressed as rage to keep others away. When Julie was seven years old her mother died, effectively pulling her family life apart. The experience created a deep fear of investing in relationships with people she might come to rely on emotionally. Like Julie's mother, that person could suddenly be taken away and deprive her of a sense of safety in the world. Julie transformed these fears into an anger she telegraphed unconsciously to others, who would respond by protecting themselves from her punching bag treatment. They avoided her. Unfortunately, these were the very others she needed to meet her goals: friendship, romance, and family. The more steam Julie let off in her self-styled "catharsis," the more people around her turned away, usually smarting from their attempts to befriend her.

Julie was an expert at rationalizing anger. In therapy she called it "catharsis." And while it's true that releasing anger feels good in the moment, it accomplishes little more than that brief jolt of relief. Short-term catharsis comes at the expense of a long-term solution, which includes not only articulating feelings, but having them responded to in a way that lets us feel heard.

Common sense says venting is a smart way to ease tension, but common sense is wrong. Upchucking our insides fans the flames. Catharsis runs interference between us and a world that may offer better ways to express emotions to people who care, rather than act them out in manners that result in others protecting themselves from us.

You may even look back now at times when you lost it, punched a wall, or threw something at someone's head and seemed to feel better. Maybe you thought it was worth being considered a dick by the person who barely dodged that plate you flung at them. The truth is, cathartically expressing your inner dick can snowball into destructive habits. Research shows that *belief* in catharsis makes one more likely to seek it out.[31] If you're convinced catharsis is healthy, you're obviously keen to indulge it. But anger begins to seem inconsequential. You vent, stay angry, and keep doing aggressive things to continue venting.

Though Julie might not mind being contradicted or rejected by her therapist, her therapist's insistence on humane treatment did set a new standard for acceptable behavior and a way of tolerating and expressing emotion that would no longer lead Julie to be abandoned by others. Julie's therapist's refusal to be a punching bag represented a significant step forward for her to be realistic about how her behavior was actually *hurting* her. Julie also found that dickery begets dickery! People prone to cathartic outbursts tend to find others who use that method, or find it intolerable when people are dicks to them and *cathart* right back when *catharted* upon.

"The yelling never worked," admitted Julie. "What's amazing is I couldn't see that until I started yelling at you. For once, rather than ducking or trying to calm me down, I was told to 'knock it off.' You shared how it made you feel, like a real person, not just a shrink. Your take on catharsis made me realize the things that actually relieve my pain in therapy—the compassion, care, openness—were stifled by the ways I sometimes act out my pain. Ways that, as you said, make me hard to tolerate."

The most effective approach to catharsis is just to stop pursuing it. Yet I don't mean an abstinence-only, "just say no" model. I'm suggesting we mindfully and thoughtfully take our anger off the burner, let it cool down from a boil to a simmer to a lukewarm state, during which we'll no longer want to scald someone. The trick is to express anger, and especially the hurt and fear underneath it, in ways that allow us to hear ourselves and recognize what we feel.

Johnny Rotten's immortal words "anger is an energy" notwithstanding, if you get into an argument, someone cuts you off in traffic, or you get called a cruel name, venting will not *energize* you, nor will it dissipate the negative energy. It will feel great, yes. Being a dick can be a blast! However, you must recognize that you'll be having fun at someone else's emotional expense. As McRaney says, "While catharsis will make you feel good, it's an emotional hamster wheel. The emotion that led you to catharsis will still be there afterward, and if it made you feel good, you'll seek it out again in the future."

This goes back to the earlier explanation of psychological defense in general. Psychological defenses protect us against awareness, but not from the effects, consequences, and influence of whatever emotional experience we are attempting to repress.

Not reacting is a big deal in dickery recovery. Scientists have even gone as far as to debunk the benefits of redirecting anger into activities like exercise. Doing this only maintains the state of increased arousal. You may even be more aggressive afterward than if you had just cooled off.[32]

It may help to think of not reacting as an action unto itself. By pausing, we withhold behavior driven by anger, hurt, and fear so we can express those emotions later in ways that are actually *heard*. It's important to note that cooling off is not the same as not dealing with the anger at all. I'm only asking that you take a time out. When you hit pause, you delay your response. Then you can relax or distract yourself with an activity that's incompatible with aggression.

Whoever Said "Misery Loves Company" Was a Dick

"Help me!" yells Valerie in the middle of the night. Her plea is intended for anyone and everyone who will listen.

To the casual observer it may seem as if this is what her therapist, yours truly, suggested she do: find and utilize her support network. No harm in that, right? But if anything, I tried to divert her and get her off my back to establish boundaries. Valerie's misery seemed to flourish the more anyone responded to her chronic state of crisis.

There are people who use the "woe is me" routine as a weapon against those who come close enough to care.[33] They are the ones who scream, *"Help me. Fix me. SOS!"* Streaming tears of indignation, Valerie believes no one cares enough to "actually do something!" It's true that her cries for help are often ignored. But that's because her pleas for assistance are often overwhelming and difficult to respond to in a legitimately helpful way.

Valerie has a good reason to feel hurt and angry. She was abused throughout her childhood and adolescence by her father while her mother turned a blind eye. Only when she was fourteen, when things got so bad the police were called, did Valerie's mother seek help, and only then because the courts required it. Ultimately, her parents divorced, mercifully separating Valerie from her abuser. But this was too little, too late.

Valerie had already internalized the message that no matter how loud you scream, how bad you ache, how much you writhe and cry for help, no one will care. She developed an obsessive-compulsive routine that caused her great misery. And she used that pain to punish anyone who tried to fool her into believing they could provide the sort of help that always eluded her. Oftentimes, these attacks were peremptory. She was especially hard on those whose role was to protect her, such as her shrink. In short, she used her misery to behave like a dick.

This behavior sabotages Valerie's career as well. She is a brilliant woman with exceptional fundraising skills, yet has lost two high-paying jobs in the past year alone. Her employment history demonstrates success, which allows her to keep finding work. But time and again she has used this destructive pattern against colleagues, bosses, top administrators, and even potential donors.

Her M.O. is this: she wields such powerful misery that all those around her offer aid. For months if not years, they bang their heads and hearts against the impenetrable wall of her gloom, quitting finally when they realize that each rescue attempt gets chewed up and spit out. It's her weapon, a version of dickery that leaves those around her wondering how, when, and where they were hit. When she feels that the jig is up, her misery having once again exhausted the resources of a support system like, say, a workplace, she'll then perceive that a boss is harassing and hurting her, making it impossible to do her work. She'll feed this fear any way she can. Constantly calling for attention, she'll tell everyone who will listen, complaining, gossiping, and attacking. In full-on obsession, she'll compulsively notify human resources, try to enlist new supporters, go to her boss's supervisor, and beyond. A momentary relief from her anxiety comes with the attention, but at a cost of having her concerns increasingly ignored or, worse, backfiring. The cycle sustains rather than diminishes her underlying anxiety.

And while Valerie may seem willing to get help, she is unable to adopt suggestions that may indeed lead to a happy mindset. Instead, she spends endless hours obsessing over everyone she believes has a better life, adhering to the maxim that, "There's no better recipe for misery than comparing my insides with your outsides."

Misery is exactly what sustains the anxiety of fear from Valerie's childhood. Coming out as dickish behavior, it protects her against "falling for it"—as in the hope that her SOS will be heard—and entitles her to lash out. Sadly, Valerie's misery also backfires by trapping her in a repetitive cycle of traumatic feelings. Remember that when the self is a weapon against the world, the self is *also* a weapon against the self.

But because her shrink was willing to challenge her attempts at catharsis, Valerie was able, through diligent hard work, to drop her attitude and express that small flicker of hopefulness hidden underneath her howling misery. Starting with expressions of sadness, hurt, and fear, Valerie loosened her conviction that the therapist would dismiss her feelings of abandonment and terror, "just like everyone else." Valerie let go of her so-called cathartic behavior and allowed herself to be cared for as a survivor of trauma, which helped heal her wounded relationship with the world.

EXERCISE: JUSTIFYING OUR DICKERY EVENT CHART

Let's look at the relationship patterns and behaviors you likely learned from your family history, focusing on experiences you recall as negative or hurtful. It will help you link past feelings of being out of control to current ones.

Event that made you feel entitled to be a dick	What you did about it (with special attention to family roles and routines)	The outcomes of your dickish reaction
Example A: My partner lost his job.	Fell into a caregiving routine where I begrudgingly took on the full burden of financial responsibility.	I felt resentful, hurt, and unappreciated. Then I seriously lessened my investment in the relationship.

CONTINUED ON NEXT PAGE

Event that made you feel entitled to be a dick	What you did about it (with special attention to family roles and routines)	The outcomes of your dickish reaction
Example B: Financial difficulties	When I had money problems I didn't let anyone else know about it or help. I stewed in resentment.	I've left relationships because I felt responsible for our poor finances.

Now, using the above examples as a reference, describe two or three of your own stressful life events that justified treating others like a punching bag. Alongside these responses, write down what you did while feeling out of control, and what the outcomes have been.

Then think about the following:

- Is there a "usual outcome" when you pursue catharsis?

- How do you react to it?

- How strong are your and others' reactions?

- Can you now see ways that these default cathartic ways of relating to others have set you up to be hurt?

- Are you able to identify the role models of these ways of expressing yourself?

- Can you imagine alternative ways of expressing rather than catharting when you feel hurt, scared, angry, or out of control?

- Might that inspire different responses from the people affected by your behavior?

- Can you imagine that expressing rather than acting out catharsis allows you to feel heard, accepted, and cared about?

PART II

DICKERY
IS
TRICKERY

CHAPTER FIVE

Everyday Dickery

Let's look at how you've been a dick. You understand the underlying reasons why people act like dicks now, so the next step is to identify when, where, and to whom you're engaged in that behavior. But first a story.

One morning on a camping trip, I noticed a gnarly-looking wasp digging a hole near our fire pit. Another dad and I discussed how much it would terrify our kids when they woke up, and how upset the wasp would be once they started playing in its territory. Eventually the other dad stood up, tentatively approached the scary insect, and stepped on the nest it had burrowed, twisting and stomping his foot. He then grabbed a log and pounded it into the dirt. After that he poured hot water down the hole and put a large rock over it.

"That takes care of that," the dad said. Yet we both had mixed feelings about what had occurred. The wasp had been minding its own business, not bothering anyone.

We had a chance to see whether these misgivings would hold up about fifteen minutes later, when the wasp popped up from a new hole in the ground, shaking dirt from its sturdier-than-we-imagined exoskeleton. Were this a cartoon, that would be the point where the wasp called in its pals or sought revenge on its own, raining stings in a blind rage against these perpetrators of evil intent. But no, our pal the wasp merely went back its super industrious life. Being dads, we couldn't help but see similarities between our actions and political events in the world. It was a huge overreaction against a perceived yet nonexistent threat.

Does this seem familiar? How many things do we worry about that never come to pass? How much of our being dicks is but a fear response?

And how often does our hostile, aggressive a-holery light off because of a fantasy of harm being done to us? Be it purely fictive, or something based on past hurt, we launch an offensive that we're convinced is a defensive stance.

When we're dicks, the world looks like a wasp. We stomp, stomp, stomp away. The wasp survived our anxious urge to protect our children and ourselves, and that's a good thing because we turned out to be wrong. The wasp didn't overreact, or react at all. We humans do much worse when we feel maligned.

You Can't Always Justify Your Actions

Like the outdated notion of catharsis, blaming others for our dickery is a losing strategy. In doing so, we ignore the most essential requirement to recover from our defensive dickery—a willingness to keep the focus on ourselves. While dicks may believe all their problems are external, as in the thinking, "It's all your fault," that attitude thwarts true healing. If everyone else is to blame for our problems, we can never get well.

Home Is Not Where the Heart Is

It's important to recognize that by being a dick, we invite the world to help us destroy ourselves. This may be as straightforward as enticing someone to beat us up. But usually the invitation is answered in more subtle ways, the worst being that no one wants to engage with us anymore. We tend not to recognize isolation as a form of destruction, yet solitary confinement is considered one of the cruelest forms of punishment. It may not be a literal isolation, however. We can become isolated in relationships with spouses, children, colleagues, and others with whom we're most familiar.

The hardest place not to be a dick is where the heart supposedly is, at home. Those intimate relationships are the ones we most often take for granted. At home, in intimate proximity, we expose ourselves to the greatest possible joys, hurts, and disappointments. When our heart gets broken by someone we love, we find ourselves suddenly surrounded by pain triggers day and night, some of which we don't even recognize as such. We replace our attempts to be liked and cared for with a vague mood of retaliation, often without even realizing it. And people begin to think we're dicks.

Subtly inconsiderate acts are another way to eat at your sense of security in your relationships. We tend to believe what our behavior implies, so if we treat certain people poorly, we eventually buy into the notion that we don't care about them as much as we had thought. This explains why toothpaste caps and toilet seats are said to be relationship killers; inconsiderate behavior not only tells our partner how we feel about them, it tells us how we feel too.

For example, my client James never kicked the habit of online flirtation, even after his partner Will shared the trauma he experienced as a kid when his father announced at the dinner table that Will's mother was having an affair. When James got caught having what Will recognized was an emotional affair, he denied it. Rather than acknowledge and deal with the lapse together, it became the elephant in the room. James didn't cease communication with his online crush, and though Will felt betrayed, he also feared making a bigger deal out of it. Try as he did, Will had a hard time convincing himself he could tolerate a betrayal so reminiscent of his past pain and loss.

They needed to resolve their different expectations regarding sexual boundaries. What didn't help was that as an adolescent, James intentionally provoked his intolerant family by trying to get caught looking at gay porn.

"I knew they found the websites, but no one said a word," James recalled. "While they were intensely vocal in their disapproval of homosexuality, they didn't try to stop me. It was confusing. I had no clue where I stood with them."

Remember, character defects start out as survival skills. In their struggle to agree upon sexual boundaries for their relationship, both James and Will reenacted unresolved conflicts from their family histories. James's unwillingness to stop his hurtful actions was an acting-out behavior. Will was being a dick by outwardly accepting James's behavior while inwardly seething instead of setting functional boundaries.

For months after James was busted, tensions increased in the house and the poor behavior on both of their parts escalated. An emotional and sexual distance hardened, which each blamed on the other. It got to a point where there was as much animosity about how they were treating each other like dicks as there was initially about James's flirtations and Will's fake tolerance.

Though we could easily convince ourselves it's James who was in the wrong, the pattern of meanness, passive-aggression, and mumbled turd hurling they developed together allowed each man to keep his heart safely out of emotional range. This was like a restraining order against working together to identify what went wrong and rebuild a sense of safety in their relationship.

For James and Will, incessant dickery worked to create a home where the heart wasn't. Each one needed the other to be honest about his feelings regarding their behavior. But the inconsiderate actions covered this up. Over the course of weeks and then months, therapy became less about who was a dick, and more about how that behavior related to the unresolved conflicts each man brought into the relationship. For both of them to feel secure and cared for, each needed to address the ways his pain and fear expressed itself. What they discovered was a deep sense of being wounded by the apathetic treatment of their respective families growing up—apathetic treatment not unlike their dickery against each other.

Regarding James's dalliances, Will said, "He doesn't care about me."

James said his acting out was a screaming effort to draw Will out of his comfort zone to save him from destroying their relationship.

Will's acceptance of James's acting-out behavior looked to him like apathy at first. Each used his own behavior, and the ambivalence it conveyed to his partner and himself, to guard against vulnerability. Each withheld empathy from the other, and neither put himself in the other's shoes to feel the havoc his emotional distance was causing. When each laid his shield of apathy down, he began to empathize with the other—understand and relate to what his lover had been through and had worked through to reach him.

Ultimately, it was the dickish behavior that highlighted the traumatic experiences each man brought into their relationship. That dickish behavior served as a cry for help that eventually enabled them to reach each other. What damaged Will and James during their respective upbringings was a lack of empathy, but they developed that bond through therapy work. Empathy may be the best cure for dickery. After all, when I put myself in your shoes and experience what you feel, the last thing I want to do is let someone act like a dick to *me*.

The End of the Honeymoon Stage

There comes a time in all relationships when we wake up and wonder if perhaps we've been kidnapped, brought to some desolate desert, dropped off, and left to die.[34] The end of the so-called *honeymoon stage* takes time to adjust to. Often it causes profound disappointment. A steep drop from the honeymoon phase can even feel like abandonment. Maybe, inspired by what had seemed like undying love, we also made an impulsive decision—we got married or had a kid—and only realize now that was about quieting our anxiety and insecurity. What then? We're deep in a relationship, and the person we're with may also feel stuck. Could it be that we were supposed to fix them and they were supposed to save us? Even though we knew better, part of us still believed in happily ever after. Now this has brought up other broken promises in our lives: unmourned losses from hopes and dreams yanked out from under us by a world incapable of following through.

Sound bleak? That's the path many of us slip down once the honeymoon phase is over. Granted, a raw deal like this can turn anyone into a dick. Many couples I work with claim that was the specific point in their relationship when bad behavior started. The disappointment and heartache around the honeymoon phase's often abrupt end feels like a betrayal. We sometimes devalue the whole relationship from then on. Often the sense of disappointment snowballs, leaving us so profoundly hurt, we go on the attack. Only in this way—and often through extremely dickish behavior—can we make our former ally, now enemy, feel the intense frustration that we feel. When the disappointment of tumbling out of the honeymoon stage infiltrates our everyday life, it's often used to justify all sorts of nonsensical acting out toward the person we believe betrayed us. And this happens in business and platonic relationships as well.

The Nuclear Snub of Work Relationships

"You know, I really hate that schmuck *Ray* in my office," Emily said. "I can't stand cowards. Ray has been a coward throughout this whole project. Thanks for helping me see that."

Come again? I thought.

Emily, Ray, and Pam are colleagues who've collaborated on a creative project over the past few years, and most of the time Emily and Ray have been allied against the supposed "authoritarian" structure Pam tries to impose. After weekly meetings, they like to commiserate about Pam's heavy-handedness. And recently, disagreements between Pam and Emily have devolved into insults and name-calling. They've both threatened to terminate the project at times as well, despite it having earned recent success.

"Not once did Ray take my side!" yelled Emily. "And yet when we talk in private, he claims to agree with me that Pam is a huge bully!"

Identifying a mutual enemy at work ushered in what felt like a new honeymoon period for Emily and Ray. They were good friends before the project started, having spent lots of time together, both one on one and with their families. For a while, the sense of camaraderie was palpable. Emily noticed, though, that their personal time had seemed to decrease in parallel to her ever-increasing tension with Pam.

"Ray says he supports me and cares about me. But he never stands up for me when Pam is bashing my brains out! The final straw was at a neighborhood picnic last week where he barely spoke to me at all. I bet I know what's going on. He's mad I invited him onto the project in the first place. It has cost us an incredible amount of time, money, and energy—to say nothing of the stress. Now, Ray's pulling back even further. I'm going to f—k him up!"

"But what actually happened?" I asked.

"Nothing! That's the problem. I'd been away for two weeks, so we had so much to catch up on, but Ray didn't ask a single question about my trip. He spent most of the time talking to the other parents and playing with the kids."

Emily's plan to blast Ray in a fit of dickery was based on a questionable interpretation of his behavior. Nevertheless, she rationalized her anger over his failure to help her process her most recent emotions about Pam, as well as the fact that he no longer acted like a starry-eyed honeymooner. Her rage would come off as a preemptive strike and surely derail their partnership right as it had begun to succeed, potentially ruining their friendship.

I sighed. "So, you plan to go nuclear?"

"Yeah," she said with a laugh.

Like many of the stories in this book, the outcome here could change dramatically if someone just took a moment to pause. This can happen naturally, when you describe the situation to someone else, like Emily did to me. You then hear how crazy your ideas actually sound.

"Okay, Doc," Emily concluded. "I see I got disappointed and began reading too much into Ray's actions. I've been seeing everything through the lens of my difficulty at work."

"So, you're not going to blast him?"

"I'm going to talk to him."

"Just don't be a dick, okay?"

"Maaaaaaaaaaaybe."

EXERCISE: AM I A DICK?

A dickish behavior I justified through someone else's behavior	How my dickish behavior was responded to	My counter-reaction/the outcome of my dickish behavior
Example A: I constantly criticized and attacked my father for his alcoholic relapses.	Dad felt ashamed each time he tried to get sober—though he was emotionally and sometimes physically abusive when he relapsed.	I increased my criticism, moved out once I could, and haven't spoken to him or my enabling mother in years.

CONTINUED ON NEXT PAGE

A dickish behavior I justified through someone else's behavior	How my dickish behavior was responded to	My counter-reaction/the outcome of my dickish behavior
Example B: My high school principal often punished me more than others (partly because we went to the same church) so I acted out and was nearly thrown out of school.	The principal said he was trying to help me and he believed I was "capable of better behavior." But I rejected his outreach and nearly wrecked my grades.	I got a very poor GPA and still struggle in educational settings, carrying forward this attitude against authority.

CONTINUED ON NEXT PAGE

A dickish behavior I justified through someone else's behavior	How my dickish behavior was responded to	My counter-reaction/the outcome of my dickish behavior

Now, using the above examples as a reference, write down two or three dickish behaviors that you justified through someone else's behavior. Alongside these responses, write down what their responses were to your dickery, and next describe the present outcomes.

After that, think about the following:

- What does your reaction to feeling mistreated suggest about the attitudes and actions you use to protect yourself?

- How does your reaction to feeling mistreated connect to your dickish behavior?

- Are you able to identify the role models of these reactions? Who taught you to protect yourself in dickish ways?

- Can you imagine different ways of behaving when you feel justified in being a dick toward others? What might that look like?

The Dick Fix

Hopefully with the awareness you've gained from answering the questions above, you're better able to see how you've contributed to the dickery that's been perpetrated upon you. And while that may feel like self-criticism, it's actually an important step. By gaining control over how we invite dickery from others, we can change the typical outcome. We're now ready to develop a more fulsome strategy—one that we'll use throughout the rest of this book and, hopefully, our lives.

1. **Hit pause.** When we're exposed to other people's dickery, it's hard to resist regressing to our mean—the average behavior we've used to protect ourselves when feeling under attack. We don't need to *resist* our knee-jerk reactions to other people's dickery so much as we just need to hit pause. At first it feels almost impossible to do nothing. But this gives us time to breathe, think, and ideally shift back to a sense of comfort with our experience before we respond. This provides a chance to consider how best to respond to other people's behavior. Many times when we give ourselves a pause, we choose not to respond at all. *I'm not going there with you* is often the most clear and salient message we can send to a dick.

2. **Take inventory.** A great sense of power over our once-reactive behavior comes once we lower our defenses and see how we've contributed to others' reactions. In pause, we take inventory of our part in an issue or problem, asking ourselves: *What was that for? What am I really trying to accomplish with this behavior? Is it getting me closer or further away from what I want in my life?* With this awareness, we spot the nuances in our behavior that affect others, and find alternative reactions. One caveat is that taking *more* than your fair share of responsibility for a problem is not the solution to a tendency to take none.

3. **Express feelings in thoughtful, deliberate ways.** In a *reaction* the action precedes the thought, while in a *response* you think then act. Therefore, to *respond* we hit pause, take inventory, and begin to express our feelings rather than act them out, which is how dickish behavior plays out.

4. **Synchronize feelings to respond rather than react.** Dickish behavior puts us at odds with the world. We often justify the behavior, unable to accept that we're at fault, and invent

narratives about being pushed into dickery by someone else. But now, with the steps we're implementing, the sense of being okay can finally line up with doing okay things.

5. **Accept ourselves and others as we actually are.** When we live in sync with who we want to be and behave accordingly, we can finally accept the limitations of others, especially dicks. Their treatment of us does not provoke a knee-jerk reaction anymore. In this way, we begin to feel comfortable in our own skin and at peace with the world.

CHAPTER SIX

Other People's Dickery

You're probably ready to shift the focus to other people's dickery and how to protect yourself from it. Sometimes it's true that it's not us, it's them. But how can we tell? That's tough, because the answer is probably the opposite of what you'd expect. We can tell someone else is the dick when we no longer feel the effects of their nasty, abusive, awful, neglectful behavior. When we build a tolerance for what is clearly maltreatment, our mind is telling us *this is too much.*

But don't worry if you can't tell whether someone in your life is an acute dick. If you haven't helped them hide it (abuse only thrives in secrecy) the fact will be conveyed by the people who actually care about you. All you have to do is listen and act upon their counsel. Would that it were so easy, I know. Being with a dick serves a less-than-conscious purpose, so it's hard to convince someone, or be convinced ourselves, that we need protection. Sure, in the midst of being abused, we hear it. We may even promise to do something about their behavior "this time." But most of us know it's extremely difficult to leave a dick. Deep down we know they're wounded because unconsciously we remember how wounded we felt when we acted that way. This brings us back to step one: the best way to avoid other people's dickery is to not be one ourselves.

The basic moves for avoiding other people's dickery are the same as they are for dealing with our own:

1. Hit pause

2. Take inventory of our part in the issue

3. Express feelings in thoughtful, insight-driven ways

4. Synchronize our feelings to respond rather than react

Here's where things differ. We need to recognize the dick's limited ability to treat us well and either:

1. Accept their dickery from afar (that is, end the relationship)

2. Let the person know our dickery is not acceptable either, and suggest working together to find better ways to treat each other

3. Accept ourselves and others as we are

Ultimately, keeping our side of the street clean is the most powerful way to protect ourselves. But this is not just about taking responsibility for our bad behavior. It's about registering our skills and virtues, and putting them to use. Often by taking care of ourselves we stay out of range of other people's bad behavior. Dicks need victims, and people who look out for themselves are not easy targets.

If you're able to process emotions and express them in healthy, productive ways, that's also likely to make it difficult to tolerate others treating you poorly. For instance, did you ever know someone who had one bad relationship after another until they put themselves in some kind of care routine like therapy or a twelve-step program? They broke out of that relationship pattern in part because allowing themselves to feel accepted as they are and cared for profoundly interfered with their tolerance of mistreatment and their availability for harmful situations. Good for them. Now it's your turn.

The Problem with Dick Tolerance

When we build a tolerance for other people's dickery, our own bad behavior becomes harder to read. We start justifying mean behavior and, emotionally stunted, we quickly get lost in defensive operations. It's sort of like building a tolerance for drugs and alcohol in that developing a tolerance for other people's dickery doesn't mean you aren't hurt by it. Using other people's bad behavior to justify ramping up your own is one way you're hurt. Even if you're unaware of it, in so-called tolerance of dickery you sacrifice a sense of self to prepare for the next bout of guerrilla warfare.

Such was the case with my client Karen. However, instead of confronting her abusive boyfriend, she turned on her best friend Hillary.

"I'm not talking to Hillary ever again," Karen said.

"What happened?"

"She promised to be there for me whenever I need her, but last weekend when Lucas flipped again, started torturing me, and threatened to kick me out—"

"Like he does every few weeks?" I inserted.

"She didn't answer my call. I called her three times."

"So, you can take nearly constant attacks from Lucas, but when your friend doesn't come to the rescue one time, you want to drop her forever?"

"It's not the first time," Karen blurted out in self-defense.

"I know. But it's also not the first time your demands have driven a friend away. A friend who, like others and like me, has been there for you numerous times when Lucas's attacks became quote-unquote 'emergencies.'"

"They *are* emergencies," Karen insisted.

"I know that too. And Hillary knows it. But when will you?" I pleaded. "At what point will you get it that he's a bad guy?"

Of course, it seems like a good idea to immunize ourselves against other people's dickery. But if our tolerance gets too high, as Karen's had, we struggle to register how, when, and if we're being hurt. Again, this emotional reaction is similar to the physiological reaction to a chemical dependency, and like the early stages of addiction, it's imperative to at least know when we're being hurt.

"I know I've said hundreds if not thousands of times that I'm leaving him after this appointment," Karen said. "But Hillary really dropped the ball this time because *this time* is different."

"*That* is what you've said hundreds if not thousands of times," I said emphatically.

When it's clear to other people that you're stubbornly staying in harm's way, the compassionate view is that this is less about masochism and more about ambivalence. What's sad, though, is that the tolerance probably draws on an early history in which you didn't have a choice about whether you would stay or go.

"Dr. B, Hillary might not believe that this is a crisis but I need you to," Karen begged.

"I believe *you* believe it, Karen," I said. "But there are several past versions of you—some fairly recent—who've asked me to remind you that we've been through this many times, and in order for you to work your way through it, we have to let you feel what's going on. Most importantly, you cannot maintain your tolerance for Lucas's abuse. The truth is, Hillary doesn't have the same tolerance for pain as you. Empathizing with you is hard for her."

"But this hurts so much."

Karen is missing the signs. But that's something she's trained herself to do. Checking out was a strategy she used to survive a chaotic childhood in which at any given time she could be abused emotionally or physically by one of her parents. Unfortunately, she brought this survival mechanism—an ability to dissociate her feelings and *not know* she was being hurt—into her adult relationships. It's only just now, with serious therapeutic work under her belt, that she's beginning to recognize what it's been like to be harmed. She's also starting to act upon this insight.

"It's supposed to hurt," I said. "Just because it doesn't consciously register as pain, doesn't mean you're not being harmed and will one day see Lucas's abusive behavior for what it is and leave."

"I believe you, Dr. B. It's just all so terrifying."

There Will Always Be Dicks at Work

How far can our dickery go toward ruining our hopes and dreams? You can get away with bad behavior for a while. But the system—be it a romantic relationship, friendship, or business—eventually kicks the dick out. Let's look at the dynamic between partners Louise, Roberto, and

Brent to see how working relationships can quickly dissolve due to poor interpersonal behavior.

The trio launched a tech start-up a few years ago. It enjoyed early success thanks in part to publicity efforts Louise and Roberto made via social media, blogs, networking, and podcast appearances. How much those efforts fueled their success remained somewhat unclear, however, which drove Brent nuts. His obsessiveness manifested in him acting like a dick. Brent treated everyone who worked for them so rudely that few of the original hires had stuck around, and without scapegoats, Roberto and Louise became targets of his ire. Brent seemed disgruntled with his back-office position, even though he'd joined the project to handle administrative duties. In lockstep with their success, he aggressively inserted himself into other areas of the company. He also acted especially miffed when Louise called Roberto their *wunderkind* in an online interview.

Louise and Roberto were technically the company's founders, and though they welcomed Brent with what they believed was immense hospitality (he'd been invited in as a full partner) Brent admitted that he entered the situation with significant concern about being "screwed." Neither Roberto nor Louise understood why he felt this way. Roberto constantly assured Brent of his value to the firm. Yet Brent's unease, which bordered on paranoia, was not assuaged by anything Louise and Roberto said. The more success they enjoyed, the more difficult Brent made things for them. One day he demanded their lawyer draw up new contracts for the group, and for each new client. Brent wanted complex proprietary agreements regarding creative elements of the business that he had little to do with. Louise and Roberto went along with it. But eventually, a major client threatened to drop their business due to Brent's insistence that lawyers revise a longstanding contract. At that point Louise and Roberto finally decided enough was enough. This was a huge account, with major ramifications for their company. But on the bright side, the crisis provided a real opportunity for Louise and Roberto to confront Brent. In the past, he'd referred to any discussion of his legal tactics as "push back." So, Louise and Roberto indeed pushed back. They argued until all three of them realized their differences were irreconcilable, at which point they agreed to break up the company.

Afterward, Louise and Roberto had a solemn resolution.

"All of this is my fault," admitted Louise, speaking just slightly tongue-in-cheek.

"I'm shocked to hear you say that given Brent's craziness."

"I know," Louise said. "But everything seemed to go awry when I called you the wunderkind."

"Well—"

"*Well* nothing," Louise retorted. "This company was our idea. We developed the branding, we found the investors, and we all but launched the thing ourselves. True, we needed Brent's skillset. But we needed him in the role he agreed to serve when we became partners. And mostly, we needed him to act like a colleague and treat us like human beings. Now after all we've spent on lawyers, the company is in debt."

"All that hard work made Brent insecure. The guy was a paranoid prick. But did we do enough to give him a sense of ownership in our success?"

"I'm not sure," sighed Louise. "It's hard to be compassionate to someone who is acting like a tyrant."

"Yes, it became the status quo to walk on eggshells to avoid upsetting him," Roberto agreed.

"What were we so afraid of?" Louise asked. "And was that really about the fine print on contracts? Like he'd actually quit?"

"Maybe in some halfhearted way we were trying to take care of him. We knew a person on edge like that had to be hurting. And yet maybe it insulted him to feel like we were trying to fix him."

"*Ugh!* Is that what we were doing? You mean we should have spent more time at work mending poor Brent's broken heart?"

"Could be," Roberto shrugged. "In truth, I don't know why we put up with him for so long. I've been trying to make sense of my own role in the fiasco. I also feel bad we let him treat the staff that way. What were we getting from him that we thought was so great?"

"Actually, if anything, Brent's manic distrust shows that we have a valuable product that you and I created together. We should keep this going without his destructive attitude. I don't know how it was for him, but for me, our success came as a shock. I wasn't prepared for it. Maybe I was superstitious about messing with the formula that coincided with our success. Our trio seemed essential to what we were achieving, especially at first."

"He was a dick then as well," Roberto said. "We can do this without him."

In the end, the client that terminated its contract during Brent's last stand returned to what went on to be a satisfying and productive business relationship in his absence. Roberto and Louise maintained their ownership stake of the company. And instead of assuming the problems they experienced were entirely Brent's fault, they agreed to be careful to address their own roles in inviting hostility into their midst. Truthfully, though, what they did wrong was continue to *tolerate* Brent's behavior after his mean, spiteful, and envious reaction to Louise's acknowledgment of Roberto's genius.

Inviting a dick into a business relationship, like Louise and Roberto did, can be a nightmare. But what happens when set ourselves up for mistreatment by the people we share our personal lives with? Such was the case with Sheila.

Sending Them Out to Sea

A client named Sheila shared a dream with me during a recent appointment. "I was in Japan, married with kids, and we lived with my parents, who were still together, but there had been a major tsunami and my whole family was washed out to sea. I was suddenly alone. I bought scuba gear—a metal helmet and a bulky underwater suit—and it was taking years, but I was determined to learn how to dive to search the sea to find them."

"Wow, you must really need time away from your family," I said, knowing something about her relationship with them.

"What?" she asked.

"The dream suggests a desire for a break! It would be the first break you've had from your family in years."

A natural-born caretaker, Sheila incessantly attracts and absorbs the calamities of others in her life. The support she gives is rarely appreciated, sadly. She is frequently taken for granted by her family and the man she is dating. Her elderly divorced parents treat her like hired help when it comes to their needs and force her to mediate their bitter disputes. Her sister has a panoply of medical issues that never seem to resolve (she doesn't follow her doctor's advice). And her boyfriend can't find adequate work.

To boot, Sheila is an advertising director who makes herself indispensable to her company by acting like the only one capable of doing her work. Simultaneously, she feels as though they treat her "like a slave."

Remember that if everyone else is to blame for our problems, we can never get well. Sheila absorbs a huge volume of dickery, which is extremely painful, yet she cannot see how the ungracious attitudes, unreasonable expectations, and the disparagements of others stem from the caretaker role she so willingly adopts. The duty she has unconsciously enacted with others calls on her to absorb their dickery, take responsibility for it, and attempt to cure it. Her hopeful notion is that someday, if the tables are turned, they'll care for her.

Sheila's responses haven't worked. At the time of her dream, it felt like the people in her life were trying to drown her. And that was how it was supposed to feel. Sheila has since worked hard in therapy to interpret her dream and learn that although the feeling was repressed and dissociated, her sincere wish was to send her loved ones out to sea and to take her time finding them.

EXERCISE: IDENTIFYING OTHER PEOPLE'S DICKERY

I'm making the assumption that if you're reading this, you've both been a dick and experienced others' bad behavior, so let's keep working. Using the following examples as a reference, write down two or three descriptions of how tolerating bad behavior wound up hurting you. Alongside these responses, explain how you managed your responses. In the last column, write down ways your tolerance for dickery came out in unexpected ways, such as acting-out behaviors that became habitual.

Other people's dickish behavior that you felt hurt by, but tolerated	How you've responded to their dickish behavior	The long-term outcome of your tolerance for the dickish behavior
Example A: My mother was constantly angry. I assumed it was due to her rough childhood.	I became my mother's emotional caretaker.	Being my mother's caretaker severely limited my career choices and romantic life until I increased my criticism of her and moved out.
Example B: My girlfriend has cheated on me many times and I've blamed myself.	I stayed with this person who makes me feel unworthy of fidelity.	My confidence is shattered and I feel like I'll never find another relationship so I remain with my partner.

CONTINUED ON NEXT PAGE

Other people's dickish behavior that you felt hurt by, but tolerated	How you've responded to their dickish behavior	The long-term outcome of your tolerance for the dickish behavior

Now, think about the following questions:

- When your tolerance has reached its limit, what happens?

- Is there a pattern that follows your feeling mistreated and justified in your dickery? A pattern to the outcome when your tolerance has worn thin?

- Can you see the cost to your overall well-being of tolerating others' bad behavior?

- Are you able to identify the role models of these reactions? Who taught you to protect yourself in dickish ways?

- Can you imagine different ways of behaving when you justify dickish behaviors in others? What might that look like?

CHAPTER SEVEN

Patrolling Dickery

Every day, we monitor other people's behavior, patrolling etiquette, just waiting for someone to be a dick. Do you walk with the flow of foot traffic? Do you let others off the bus before pushing your way on? Do you text while walking? Do you drive aggressively? Do you ever take those ear buds out? Do you ride your bike against the flow of traffic on the street—what we call *salmoning*? There are many rude offenses people commit in public. If it's not clear by now, I can tell you that these are my own pet peeves.

When someone does something we consider wrong, we use it as an excuse to bombard them with dickery. Because some of these exchanges allow us to remain relatively anonymous, we feel entitled to them. For example, it seems justified to mumble obscenities at someone who nearly bumps into us with the two big dogs they're walking up Broadway in rush-hour pedestrian traffic. We may even believe this person is not just a dick to her fellow humans, but to the dogs as well. But oh how things change when it's our dog who meanders in front of people on the sidewalk!

According to traditional psychoanalytic theory (that would be Freud and his acolytes), we have a police officer in our head—a *superego*—that tells us how to behave and reinforces our rules and regulations by making us feel guilt and shame when we fail to live up to our own standards. The superego is recognized as a paternal authority internalized by resolving the Oedipus complex. Overwhelmed by the power expressed by our opposite-sex parent, we choose to take in their authority rather than fight it. This is known as the First Law of Power, and it looks a lot like what happened in the last chapter between Louise and Brent when she called Roberto a wunderkind. As Robert Greene explains it in *The 48 Laws of Power*: "Always make those above you feel comfortably superior. In your desire to please or impress them, do not go too far in displaying your talents or you might accomplish the opposite—inspire fear and insecurity. Make your masters appear more brilliant than they are and you will attain the heights of power." Greene refers to this tactic simply as, "Never Outshine the Master."[35]

How is it that these internal superego spankings ("I've been a naughty kid") go from reeling in our bad behavior to excusing it? You'd think that a superego, another term for your *conscience*, would help you get along with others. We all need a voice of reason in our head to tell us to do this and not that, and to keep our pride, narcissism, and entitlement in check.

The funny thing is, though, the therapeutic work entailed in dealing with the superego tends to be less about beefing it up and more about tamping it down. Rather than resulting in good citizenry, the severe force of our guilt and shame over doing things wrong negatively impacts our self-esteem, confidence, and efficacy. Feeling like a "bad person" because of nagging remorse is unlikely to make us "good people" when it's continually bubbling up. In fact, when we feel bad about ourselves we tend to look for external reasons why. *Who did this to me?* we wonder. *How can I feel better?* Rather than take a hard look within, our search for answers leads to scapegoats, a guilty verdict projected by our superego indictment.

In this way, our development comes with built-in means to justify our dickery. With a great capacity to protect ourselves from things we don't want to know about ourselves, we end up rationalizing all kinds of behavior that does, in actuality, invite punishment in the form of rejection, withdrawal, aggression, and abandonment from others.

So, when we feel guilty about our bad behavior, our minds can protect us from bad feelings and stunt the process of changing that behavior. Instead of feeling remorse—which might actually help us become better people—we instead get riled up when we see someone else do the same thing.

And to be clear, while we might not feel bad about doing something rude, it's unlikely to feel good when we're called out by others. People still see us acting like dicks and sometimes communicate those qualities we try to hide from ourselves to us through counterattacks.

While any form of dickery can piss people off and put laser sighting dots on our heads, impulsive reactions to other people's alleged breaches of etiquette during everyday life are among the sorts of behaviors most likely to result in violence. In these moments we risk shining a light on a quality the other person doesn't want to accept or know about themselves. For instance, that woman wasn't being ungracious when she didn't thank you for holding the door, she was just distracted, caught up in some other concern. Your sarcastic *"you're welcome"* caught her attention, however. It made her question her manners, but instead of acknowledging the lapse, now she wants to slap you. So many things we feel entitled to, like one little remark to let someone know their faux pas has annoyed us, and the next thing we know we're in a screaming match, pounding on a car horn or shouting in the face of a person who likewise wants us off the planet.

A client of mine once said he commented "in a friendly way" on a passing pedestrian's "salmoning," so the guy followed him for several blocks spewing words that definitely need *impletives* as he also questioned my client's manhood. This *impletive* concept—using replacement language for something too obscene or crass to be spoken—might be what being a dick is all about.

To be a dick is to use others as a stand-in for bad feelings about ourselves. An impletive captures those things we need and *need not* say. A profound service, therefore, is provided in the process of creating and filling in these blank spaces—it allows us to distance ourselves from others and how we think and feel about ourselves.

Maybe when we're tempted to offer unsolicited advice to people on the street, it would help to suddenly imagine them as 250-pound land sharks. After hitting the pause button, we can then ask ourselves, "What should I say *now*?"

Nothing. And that's the point. By easing up on others and accepting ourselves, we pave the way for a less hostile world.

There may be moments, though, when we use up all of the leeway around us, tolerance, patience, and understanding having been exhausted. If your history is full of bad behavior, it can be especially hard to recognize that you're acting like a jerk. We can distinguish dickish behavior in others, but remain unable to see it in ourselves.

Victimless Dickery? There's No Such Thing

Sometimes bad behavior is rationalized by some version of the phrase, "There are no victims, only volunteers." I suppose if you believe that, then the ramifications of such behavior—gnawing guilt, shame, and soul-sickness—don't worry you. Then again, many dicks wake up in a different head than the one they went to bed with. Feelings break through that claim it's you, not the unsuspecting partner of the dude you've been scrogging, who is the victim. Or excuse me, *volunteer*.

A few more dick-defending chestnuts are, "No one got hurt," "What she doesn't know won't hurt her," and the crème de la crème, "He deserved it." Keep telling yourself that and maybe someday you'll be convinced. And how good do we really feel when such behaviors become habitual, compulsive, and out of our conscious control?

Dickish behavior boomerangs and hits its perpetrator in the heart, leaving he or she in isolation. There is simply no victimless dickery, as no one who participates in it goes unscathed.

The Impletive in Action

I was running on a path along the East River with my daughter, Uta, in a jogging stroller. My older daughter, Kata, rode next to us on her bicycle. And as we came to a turn in the path, another cyclist who appeared to be a deliveryman sped by and came dangerously close to hitting us. It startled me, and for a moment I was mad.

The delivery guy must have felt the same way. He turned around and hurled a string of curses at me for jogging in the bike lane.

Enraged, I felt the urge to chase him down and fight. But I didn't. The deliveryman slowed to continue cursing me out. So, to interrupt the vulgarity he was exposing my kids to, and to talk back (though we know catharsis is flawed), I barked nonsense at him. "CHAAA-CHOOO-CHAA, blah-blah-blah." It was a knee-jerk reaction, done with no more conscious purpose than to make noise. That odd impletive use seemed to distract, confuse, and ultimately defuse the situation.

"Expletive, expletive, expletive," he had said.

"Impletive, impletive, IMPLETIVE," I responded. I smiled. Then my older daughter giggled and my younger daughter followed suit.

Alas I cannot say he laughed, or made anything approximating a friendly gesture. He simply rode off.

"What did he say, Daddy?" Kata asked.

"I'm not sure," I lied.

"What did you say?"

"Nothing." I answered. Though that wasn't precisely accurate, since by speaking in gobbledygook with a smile and two cute kids in tow, I expressed something so goofy it became pretty freaking hard to follow through on my aggression.

Was I a dick? In that guy's mind, certainly.

Was he? You could argue as much, but when Uta asked me, "What happened?" I'd cooled down enough to realize, "We scared that guy. He thinks we almost caused him to crash."

"Oh."

My use of the impletive was not some savvy concept or practice drawn from my work as a psychoanalyst. It had more to do with protecting my kids from obscenities while not wanting them to see me act out. It served as a *pause* button, fortunately, and that's exactly what I hope to install for you.

Everyday Rage

John is a self-described "good guy" who will nevertheless slide into dickery whenever strangers fail to live up to his code of etiquette on the street. He's not above bumping into people blocking the subway doors, whispering curses, or yelling at people who ride their bikes on the sidewalk.

Although he's a busy professional, he prides himself on taking time off during the week to "be a good daddy," yet when his kids are with him his behavior can be even more outlandish. Somehow pushing a stroller or getting the kids in a cab makes other people's misbehavior more disturbing. So as much as he loves the daddy role, it wears him out. Like me with my daughters, he feels compelled to be a dick, but conflicted about showing that side of himself.

One day, John took the kids to a free concert in a park downtown. It was a hot summer day, and when they got there the concert had been cancelled due to the heat. John had brought the kids in a massive, unwieldly stroller. It was like a tank. With one kid dangling from its perch, and the other inside, John—sweaty, tired, and pissed-off—trudged through the subway system ready to explode.

As luck would have it, the elevator was broken at their subway stop. John had to haul the monster stroller up the stairs, his two kids groaning, but halfway up he saw a woman coming down *the wrong way*, on John's side of the handrail, obstructing their path. In his mind, she was either inconsiderate or stupid.

This time, John wouldn't bother withholding his rage. With each step he planned his attack. Then just when he was ready to lambast her, she increased her pace, which gave him *pause*, and without a word lunged down to grab ahold of the front end of the stroller to help him lug it up the rest of the stairs.

I love this story because it shows that while hitting pause doesn't necessarily save us from dickish thoughts, it does give us the opportunity to not act on them. In that way, we'll occasionally see the world is not the bad place we thought it was.

EXERCISE: IMPLETIVE

I'm inviting you to take what I'm calling the impletive—the *!@#%*— and use it like the classic Rorschach inkblot test. In response to the question, "What do you call yourself?" one might reply, "I'm a dick." The impletive allows you to find your own way of expressing feelings about others and yourself. There are so many good, powerful, effective, provocative, offensive, or benign words we can use to refer to troublesome people and behaviors.

The reason I'm suggesting alternative language choices is to help you take it easy on yourself and accept who you are, and who other people are. When we lower the offense level of the word we use to describe ourselves at our worst, we pave the way toward a less hostile world.

So, along with the transformation of any *agreements* we've made between the world and ourselves, we might let our mind romp and bounce about as it lands upon this word and that to fill in the blank as we seek descriptors for the kind of people we are. It may wind up being more difficult to use words that are kind and generous than it is to be obnoxious and mean. But no one said getting better would be easy.

Being a dick has been a powerful way to be closed off, shielded against the harm others can do to us when we're vulnerable. The new agreements we're developing between ourselves and the world pose a threat to these well-established defenses, however, and an impletive can create needed space for growth by helping us let go of the hostile attitude.

Without overthinking it, write down a few new words you can substitute for #@!%—the term you use to describe a total dick:

1. _____

2. _____

3. _____

Are these milder impletives than the ones you used for the exercise in Part 1? I hope so.

Bottoming Out

They say the bottom is where you put the shovel down and stop digging. It's up to you to decide how hurt you need to be before you give up your bad behavior. Often this aligns with the point at which you recognize you're a dick. You feel bad about it, and remorse provides the will to change.

So, have you hit bottom yet? Are you ready to stop digging?

If so, keep reading. If not, keep reading anyway. Some people take longer to hit bottom than others, and some never do. We all know people who've burned through marriages, familial relationships, and jobs. Some of these individuals may have also done prison time, stayed in psychiatric hospitals, or been to emergency rooms after fights—yet still don't budge behaviorally. In fact, some people own their irascibility and think being called a "dick" is a badge of honor. Until they feel the emotional consequence of their behavior, there's not much hope for change.

Take my client Julian. Back in the 1990s he was in the grunge scene, rode a motorcycle, wore ripped jeans, and prided himself on being a dick. His attitude attracted punishing reactions, and his behavior usually led to ill consequence for others as well.

Julian called himself a "heat-seeking missile" and had a knack for choosing the exact wrong person to hurl his arrogance upon. He was also one of those good-looking bad boys who attracted just the wrong type of partner. There's a psychoanalytic tenet that "we know more than we know we know," which is a clever way to say there are unconscious reasons we're drawn to a particular type of person, and that person is drawn to us.

One night, Julian went to a small Orange County club to see a then little-known Seattle band called Soundgarden. He arrived tipsy—his many dick moves that night included driving under the influence—and beelined it to a cocktail server.

Julian sensed that she thought he was cute, but since he was inebriated, his follow-through bordered on assault. The gargantuan bouncer, who happened to be the waitress's boyfriend, saw the entire interaction and grabbed Julian by his jacket, pulling him off and away from the unreceptive waitress. Then what did Julian do? Can you guess? He swung at the dude who was twice his size and who had him lifted off the floor.

Luckily for Julian, the professional duties of a bouncer did not include pummeling the shit out of unruly concertgoers. He did, however, launch Julian out the door.

Sitting on his butt, Julian decided he wasn't done with the club, or the bouncer, or the waitress. He went to his motorcycle, put on his helmet, ran full speed back to the club, and took a flying leap at the bouncer.

Fortunately, the bouncer restrained from putting Julian in the hospital or the grave, and instead hurled him down onto his backside a couple more times in the parking lot. So, while Julian was lucky to survive the boomerang effect of his dickery, he was not so lucky in that he went on to engage in more situations that took him to the brink of getting his ass kicked enough to learn his lesson, but not quite there.

In other words, a more violent tussle might've led to the revelation that some kind of personal change was necessary.

Agreements Redux

Insight is at the core of the analytic process, yet insight without work is worthless. You are now in a position to do something with what you've learned—transform insight into action. Let's return to what I call our "agreements." The most important thing we've learned about them so far is that most of us don't recognize they exist. Now that we do, let's turn them into something useful—a vision of ourselves comfortable in our skin and at peace with the world.

Go back to the original agreements you wrote down in Chapter One and consider what it's like to act on them versus what it's like to resist them, and come up with alternative agreements.

EXERCISE: AGREEMENTS

Agreement	How this agreement influences my behavior toward others	How this agreement results in me being a dick
Example A: Since I'm the only who provides care in the relationship, I get to decide what we do together on the weekends.	When I feel burdened and resentful about my caretaking role, I discover I have an agreement to take charge of other areas of our lives.	My family now declines my help saying "the price is too high" and I'm "controlling." I feel more isolated and alone.
Example B: If I go out of my way to accept whatever others offer me (whether it's what I really want or not), I feel entitled to complain about it.	When I accept other's questionable behavior, but they don't accept mine, I feel a right to vent. I'm told this agreement seems like gossiping.	When my complaining gets misperceived as gossip, the people I vent to distance themselves as if I'm untrustworthy.

Now, using the above examples as a reference, write down two or three of your own *agreements* with the world. These could be the agreements you've used before, or ones you've excavated through the previous exercises. Then answer the following questions:

- How rigid are these agreements—and the attitudes and actions that go with them?

- Is it possible that these agreements have put you in a position to be hurt?

- Might the transformation you are seeking come from changing the agreements that exist between you and the world? What might that look like?

PART III

HOW
TO
QUIT

CHAPTER EIGHT

You're Already Okay

Congratulations on making it to the recovery section of the book. Living in harmony with the world is a daily reprieve. You get the moment-to-moment experience of being at peace in your own skin. You drop your guard, making it easier to accept yourself, others, and the circumstances you face as they actually are. And you're not under constant attack, because you're acting gentler.

Being a dick has placed you in a position to be hurt, you realize. As the "Big Book" of Alcoholics Anonymous states, so long as we keep our eyes open and watch where we step, we're less likely to "step on the toes of our fellows" and trigger their retaliation. With this attitude, the world becomes a more hospitable place. We just need to understand that *being okay*—my phrase for living at peace with ourselves and others—is the proverbial "inside job." It's not a matter of hoping everyone else behaves.

You're already equipped to be okay. Choosing to read a book about bad behavior and paying attention to your psychological tendencies proves it. You don't need to be in situations anymore that compel you to be a dick. That won't make you feel better—you're already okay. You just need solutions to maintain this new commitment.

Turning Trust on Its Head

We often justify acting like a dick through distrust of other people. But in my experience, most dicks *do* trust others. They trust other people will attack and hurt them. What they don't realize—because they keep thinking, *I don't trust them*—is that the trust they have in how corrupt other people are confines those individuals to dickish responses. Trust, after all, is a sense that we establish over time. After enough experience with someone we believe that they will operate exactly the way they tend to. So, when it comes to dicks and dickish behavior, they need to turn this notion of trust in more positive direction.

A client of mine named Joaquin once mused, "With each failed relationship I built a case against love, care, and support—even though those were things I wanted—and I had no clue I was reviving a rationale from my childhood to trust no one, ever."

Like many people do, Joaquin figured out that when we rationalize dickery as our default setting, we turn the common notion of trust into a permanent mode of distrust. Being a dick becomes our SNAFU (Situation Normal: All F—ked Up). People respond to our rudeness in due form. And we come to "trust" that this is how the world works—people treat us like crap. If we're bona fide dicks, we never see our part in their response.

Our culture traditionally attaches the term "trust" to people and institutions we confidently rely on, yet when we're dicks, or if we live with other people's dickery, we learn to trust only ourselves. Our life experiences serve as data showing that people are exactly who we fear them to be. Since that perception is crafted by disappointing, painful experiences, we take our trust away from all individuals and put it on our anxiety toward relationships in general. It's no surprise then that we "trust" unequivocally that relationships are doomed to fail and generally frustrate us.

"I choose to date the same type of person again and again," continued Joaquin. "And each time I fall for a woman, I struggle to handle her. I guess I'm attracted to people who need my understanding and care. That makes me feel good about myself. Eventually, though, they reject me, which reminds me of what it was like to live with miserable parents who couldn't be cheered by anything I did. They treated me like dirt. I grew up learning to survive intolerable treatment, but it's still hard to accept that every time a romantic partner rejected me, it actually shows that I trusted them to do that."

We build walls against our awareness of experiences that disprove our belief that others will fail us. We establish basic *trust* in the failures of early childhood relationships. Parents who didn't provide safety, for example. And these are convincing lessons of what we can expect in the future. With each relationship, Joaquin gathered more assuredness that people were coldhearted, and that he should trust his instincts about them the next time around. He believed he needed to protect himself *and* continue to recognize where emotional dangers lurked.

Being a dick, or believing we're okay with other people's dickery, also requires trust that we'll inevitably fail and disappoint people. Statisticians call this *regression to the mean*—a guarantee that given enough opportunities, things return to their average state. If you tend to lie, it's likely that despite the occasional anomaly of honesty, you'll once again lie more often than not. When we're in an adversarial relationship with the world, we use this "trust" principle to justify our behaviors and belief that relationships are only reliable in that they always let you down.

Breaking this skeptical pattern requires developing a new mean to regress to. I told Joaquin he needed a new default setting. One that didn't constantly trigger counterattacks from others.

"I *would* like to stop trusting in negative results," Joaquin admitted with a sigh.

Working Through It

Halting negative assumptions about people and circumstances is necessary to heal. In fact, breaking trust, in the distrustful sense of the word, is a crucial step in breaking out of our rigid patterns of putting ourselves in harm's way. Therapists call this process *working through*. It involves attaining insight into our tendencies to use dickery to protect ourselves from vulnerability and accepting that this isn't working. These epiphanies can convince us to reconsider and reframe *trust*, and stop wasting our time repeating patterns that don't work. Attaining a better understanding of the ins and outs of our best-defense-is-a-good-offense way of relating to the world allows us to hit pause when tempted to react hurtfully to others' behavior. In sum, we get into a habit of making the time and space necessary to develop responses that aren't hostile, knee-jerk reactions. Thus, we break our previously held trust that others intend to hurt us.

As we progress, we realize that when we drop our negative point of view, personal interactions are unencumbered by the past. Instead of continuing with the same old frustration, we sever that compulsion that wound up hurting us.

Working through gets all that gunk out of our system. We need to let go of the toxic waste we've used to excuse bad behavior. Think of it like having an illness; you apply all available home remedies, rest, drink plenty of water, and do whatever else is in your power to clear the infection, up to and including seeing a doctor.

In a sense, it's simple: we need to acknowledge, own, and express what had been previously acted out in bad behavior. This allows us to drop our dickish behavior and embrace the risks that come with receiving compassion, understanding, and care. In doing so, we can make genuine connections with others and exorcise those dissociated, repressed parts of ourselves. Sincere personal connections heal the isolation and loneliness that all too often drives our dickery. We experience ourselves more fully.

Since our psychological defense system protects us from anxiety triggered by people, any process that renews access to the range of emotions these defenses mask must also include people.

Typically this process is *enacted,* or played out, in conversations with a shrink in therapy. But since you're not being sent to therapy (or at least not yet!) you can allow the outside world to interpret your actions for you as you work through your dickish history and clear out those stubborn remnants of your *present.* Because, yes, we want to halt these outdated ways of protecting ourselves and heal the damage caused to our relationships *now.*

The point is to be able to see ourselves—how we guard against others and our own anxieties—from a new perspective, so that, should we choose to, we can change our dynamic with the world one relationship at a time. The fact is, being a dick only allows for a narrow vision of the world and our place in it.

Know Your Rights

Remember to take responsibility for your actions. You have a right to take credit for the things you said or did that were *right.* Don't let it go to your head, though. We've already noted the difference between being right and being *righteous*. And the most important thing is to take responsibility for actions that were wrong.

This is not a popular approach in our culture, but let's be unequivocal here—without owning your mistakes you disregard the future health of your relationships. That's like throwing your hands up in the driver's seat as your car speeds toward the edge of a cliff, symbolically saying, "Nothing I can do about that!"

People say we're "powerless over people, places, and things," and for the most part I agree. However, when you claim innocence for what goes on in your relationship, you disavow responsibility for harms done and lose the power to fix what is wrong—your part of it.

Dicks believe any admission of wrongdoing is an opening to be hurt. Yet through these humble admissions, we loosen our rigid fear that the world will always mistreat us. Allowing ourselves to be wrong—taking responsibility for our part in problems or conflicts—offers a chance to *work through* and:

- See and feel your dissociated emotions

- Do something constructive about your role in the problem

- Enjoy the satisfaction of knowing your anxiety toward others can be overcome

While scary at first, this work is immensely empowering. Now when things go wrong in a relationship, instead of only contributing to the problem, we can be part of the solution as well. Defending ourselves, being dicks, and devaluing others aren't the only options available anymore. We learn that *yes*, sometimes relationships fall apart. But each conflict can also be an occasion to strengthen our bonds by working together to put things back together.

A Moratorium between Your Rage and the World

Calling a moratorium on acting like a dick allows you to respond more appropriately. Hitting pause is not a cure in itself, but rather a strategy to avoid acting out, and to see the world is not the bad place we think it is. For instance, Monday after Monday Joan plops herself down on my couch to complain bitterly about the most recent "email battle" she's had with her sister.

Joan and her sister share the caretaking responsibilities for their elderly mother. Each one does the majority of the care one week, and the other takes over the next. The exchange occurs on Sunday evenings, via email, and just about always leaves Joan reeling with anger and resentment.

"It's not easy to explain to my sister what's gone on when I look after my mom," Joan said. They began using email after months of heated face-to-face meetings and phone calls. But every form of communication with her sister is met with disdain.

The feelings Joan expressed in therapy began with rage, but when she felt safe, she revealed that these exchanges saddened her. "They make me feel like I'm being a bad daughter," she added. "I compare myself with Sherry and feel like I don't measure up. It fills me with remorse and regret, and I think these emotions are caused by what Sherry says."

"What does she say?" I asked.

"Funny," admitted Joan, "it's not anything overtly provocative or accusatory. I just feel like there's a tone to her emails—like she's being judgmental about my care. And she reacts the same way to me."

"Did you ever consider seeing what happens when you *don't* hit send? I mean, go ahead, write whatever you feel—all the hurt, rage, all that—then send it to yourself. See what happens. Wait 'til Monday, maybe even until after our session, and see if you still want to send it."

So, she did. And within the next few weeks, instead of raging at each other, Joan and Sherry began to discuss how sad and scared they are about losing their mother. They also showed regret and remorse for their earlier fights, and acknowledged a guilt-ridden sense that they wished they could do more for their mother. Since they're no longer dissociating these uncomfortable emotions, they express them in ways that can be heard. Sometimes they even discuss their gratitude to be able to share these feelings with each other.

By hitting pause, Joan took a step toward *working through* her anxiety rather than knee-jerk react to her sister's tone. It led to new ways of relating to Sherry and to herself, because she was no longer triggering hostility from her sister. Being aware of what we're up to—how we act out uncomfortable or intolerable feelings—allows us to develop and refine more functional ways of expressing ourselves.

Being truly heard requires sincere communication, which is unlikely when people defensively protect themselves. More thoughtful ways of expressing ourselves help others drop their guard, exchange heartfelt attention, and eventually deliver the kind of care we all deserve from normal human interaction.

For instance, before I send an angry email I ask myself, "Does it need to be said that way? Do I need to say this right now? Does this message have to come from me?"

These are *hit pause* questions. Like I suggested to Joan, whenever I compose an email with a hint of anger or acrimony, I hit send—but only to myself. This is an agreement I've made with myself and the world. I let as much time pass as needed before I revisit the email to reassess its merit. The results are that I either:

1. Send it as is (a rare event)

2. Send it after scrubbing out the dickery (a middle ground that's probably my most frequent choice)

3. Don't send it at all, after which I'm grateful I resisted the impulse to lash out aggressively like I did that one time at 5:30 a.m. (*ugh*)

The Romeo Walkout

There's no place that we're more likely to act out our uncomfortable feelings in knee-jerk ways than in a long-term relationship. When someone has the potential to love and accept us as we are, it terrifies us. But hitting pause allows us to reassess what's going on in a volatile interaction *and* keep our relationship from going off the rails.

"For that terrible year after our honeymoon phase, I wasn't sure we would make it," began Ben. "One day we were progressing to the next level by becoming proud parents of Romeo, our bulldog, then the next was like *wham*—full of disappointment and rage. Every time I was hurt or angry, I'd take Romeo and leave, sometimes for more than an entire day."

Matteo chimed in, "I'd plead with him to tell me what was wrong. And I never knew if he'd come back."

As we know, being a dick is sometimes a reaction to feeling vulnerable. That loss of control over our feelings threatens us. And at no time is this more intense than in a romantic relationship; the love for our partner takes over, and when insecure, shanghais us in a realm of uncontrollable emotion. No amount of assurance—not extra doses of lovemaking, weekends holed up in our love nest, pledges of utter devotion, or a puppy named Romeo—can remedy the fact that what would really make us feel better would be to run away.

So while it's hard to fault Matteo for thinking Ben acted like a dick, a nuanced reading of the situation would delve into his complicated backstory. Ben's family nearly disavowed him for his homosexuality, stating throughout his youth that they "hate the sin, but not the sinner," a claim he always found unconvincing.

When Ben hit the dating scene in college, he brought with him an internalized homophobia, and although it was a far more tolerant setting than Ben's hometown, he felt unable to value anyone who accepted and cared about him. Using a cold shoulder as a form of heart-protection, he blocked himself from love and from being loved. Continuing this pattern would've ensured his emotional safety, but it would have also come at the expense of the happiness offered by loving relationships. The pattern of loneliness and isolation that he used to protect himself from his parents' bigotry lasted this way for years. Eventually though, after significant therapy, Ben told me he felt "prepared" for love. But was he really?

When Ben walked out on Matteo, he was expressing that he needed a break. So, was it okay to leave when his heart pounded like it was about to explode through his chest? That depends.

Hitting pause and calling a moratorium on hot-tempered reactions takes a behavior that often poisons romantic relationships (stonewalling) and transforms it into a productive episode in which we take care of ourselves. We can include our partners in this by discussing the use of a pause when we're not in a moment of conflict, agreeing upon it as an alternative to stonewalling and freezing each other out. I find that using a pause in consensus allows us to feel supported by our partners as well; they're assenting for us to take care of ourselves and our relationship.

When we call for a pause or a break instead of imposing one on others,[36] we might find that the destructive interactions stop. We do this by dropping an inflammatory topic for an agreed upon time—be it fifteen minutes, an hour, or a whole day. Detaching from one another's company for that time can also help.

Our moratorium is not the same as what the Gottmans call "stonewalling"—it's the opposite. Stonewalling is the harsh, selfish punishment of simply not talking to a partner for an undisclosed period of time (what some call "the silent treatment"), whereas a moratorium is an *agreed upon* pause to develop a productive response as soon as you have more positive attitudes. The key to establishing a productive moratorium process is to come up with a way to implement it; this strategizing is best done when you and your significant other are in a calm, allied mood. That way, when things aren't going well, you have set process to separate, gather your thoughts, and come back together to deal with the issue. A good rule of thumb is to return to the conflict when the warmth of the relationship has returned. Of course, the two of you will have to feel out when you're both ready to discuss your respective roles in the issue.

Either person can request—not demand—a moratorium, which ends when both are ready for it to end.

Because Matteo and Ben had agreed to use a moratorium when things felt heated, Ben's walkout was seen as a necessary pause that would allow him to take a break, recharge, and return, rather than a "f—k you," as it had been in his previous relationships.

With this practice, we're not only *a lot* less likely to act like dicks, we're less likely to be perceived that way.

A Better Way to Take a Verbal Break

We've seen how a moratorium, a break that's agreed upon, can take what might otherwise be a death knell for a relationship (stonewalling) and transform it into breathing room to avoid impulsive and destructive behavior. We can't force a reconciliation until both of us are ready to repair. And sometimes the road to agreeing upon this kind of mutual pause is bumpy. But most of us can pull it off if we give ourselves and our relationships the chance.

"Don't tell me I've stepped on one of your landmines again," Carter moaned. "Molly, what did I do?" She didn't answer. "So now you're giving me the silent treatment?"

There's hardly a more dickish move in relationships than the *freeze out*. We're all tempted to storm out of places, even extremely intimate ones, because we don't know how to process our vulnerability or express it in a productive way. But what about occasions when we storm out without actually doing so? Unfortunately, silent rage has much the same effect as aggressive rage. What if we transformed that passive-aggressive move into something productive?

It's hard for Carter not take it personally when Molly gives him the cold shoulder. But he shouldn't. Molly grew up in a tumultuous household; her parents constantly screamed at each other, and once Molly's siblings were old enough, they joined the fight. The soundtrack to her childhood was a cacophony of tantrums and yelling, occasionally followed by the smacks and cries of physical violence. Checking out and shutting down—a form of dissociation—was how Molly survived the mayhem in her family life.

Silence is dangerous because often it's interpreted as a personal rebuke to shut someone out completely. But when we look a bit deeper, we see that silence is often used to cover up the desperate need to escape what feels like an escalating confrontation. This type of silence nevertheless causes others to feel rejected and abandoned. It's a lose-lose situation in that both people feel hurt.

It's just so difficult to hit pause and remain calm when our feelings are hurt. Suggesting some other way to be, however, is also challenging. So, what if we looked at the space one person requests (as opposed to *demands* or *imposes*) as a shared space either person can call for at any time? And what if we use this space to build assurance that *going away* emotionally for an agreed upon time is dramatically different than rejection or abandonment?

Very calmly, Molly and Carter discussed their needs in session with me and agreed to give pausing a chance.

They discovered that even in the best relationships, individuals can need a break from one another when things get heated. It allows you to mutually retreat from a crisis that feels out of control. Having taken a few steps back allows the warmth of the relationship to return, and our good feelings for each other help us regain a state of balance. The moratorium offers space not only to calm dickish behavior, but also to convert that next critical moment in the debate into a choice made in partnership, together. What can't be overemphasized is that the space is mutually agreed upon rather than imposed, wielded, and smashed upon our heads in the form of freezing out.

Neither Carter nor Molly have to walk away from their disagreement feeling bad. A moratorium now allows them to see that silence need not be dickish, nor is interpreting our partner's behavior as such necessary or accurate.

It's Time for Personal Empowerment

Accounting for and taking responsibility for our contributions, good and bad, to a relationship is the cornerstone of empowerment. Without accountability, you remain at the mercy of the actions (many of which, if you're a dick, are counter-reactions) of those around you. Taking responsibility requires an awareness of what hurts us, what scares us, and how we've reacted to emotional pain and fear historically. With this awareness, we can now *see* and *feel* the injuries rather than react to them with bad behavior. This means being able to respond to the world rather than react—no longer at the mercy of our defensiveness toward things that hurt us. There may come a time when you realize being called "sensitive" is payoff for the hard work of recovering from dickery. It means you know where you hurt.

The only legitimate power to change your dickery comes from knowing what you're up to when you behave badly. The best way to decode yourself, as we'll see, is through *inventory*. Keep the focus on yourself to discover what the dickishness is about, what it actually expresses, and how it manifests in behaviors and relationship patterns. In inventory, we can take responsibility for our part in the trouble we have when engaging with the world. Inventory begins once we've established a willingness to do something about our struggles with others and with ourselves. Then comes the action part, when we stop being a dick!

EXERCISE: WHAT WORKS

Are there solutions you've found to deal with being a dick? What are they? If you found effective ways to work through your problems, but haven't used them on a regular basis, what might the reason for that be? Are you resistant to a better relationship with the world? List solutions that might work and discuss ways to commit to them as a foundation for empowerment:

1. _____

_____

_____

_____

2. _____

_____

_____

_____

3. _____

_____

_____

_____

EXERCISE: TRANSFORMING DICKERY INTO EMPOWERMENT

Inventory, as I am using it, is the process whereby we account for our contribution to whatever problems, issues, or conflicts we're having. Usually, these issues are in significant relationships, such as with a spouse or family member, or in our environment (at work, especially). Inventory involves:

1. Careful consideration of your part in the problem or conflict,

2. Thoughtful assessment of the motivations and underlying thoughts or feelings that your behavior expressed,

3. A record of your understanding (often written down), and

4. An acknowledgement of your accountability to someone else.

A "spot-check" inventory is a similar process, but the timeframe is much shorter and we use it to account for, take responsibility, and ideally cease a potentially destructive behavior *right now*. In a spot-check, we still ask the question "what's my part in this?" and consider our feelings and motivations. But unlike the formal inventory, which is generally used as a means of understanding and changing chronic, often addiction-related behavior, the spot-check inventory is a process to stop what you're doing anytime you feel yourself drifting into dickish behavior.

Think of it as another way to hit pause before reacting to something someone said or did that hurt you, scared you, freaked you out, or pissed you off. In that pause, you can account for your part in the issue at hand and assess possible solutions. Choose a problem—preferably a recurring issue that has historically justified your dickery—and start your own spot-check inventory. You can use this model to address issues as they arise.

• THE ISSUE_____

Who was hurt and the nature of this harm	How I justified not addressing my role in it	My feelings about the harm I've done	How I've attempted to repair it and the result

If there is someone with whom you can work on the following chart, take an inventory of your relationship together and explore how being a dick has interfered with the sense of safety and security between you. Use these results as a model to deal with issues as they arise.

• THE ISSUE/CONFLICT _____

How you each felt hurt, scared, or upset	How you each justified the harm and avoided addressing your role in the problem	Your feelings on having harmed each other and the relationship	How you each tried to repair the harm, and the results so far

EXERCISE: AVOIDING MUTUALLY ASSURED DESTRUCTION BETWEEN YOU AND THE WORLD

The next exercise will provide awareness of common couple pitfalls. Use this knowledge to assess your relationship patterns and codevelop ways to see conflicts as windows of opportunity and cries for help. Developing alternatives to being a dick will help you quit isolating from each other as well.

First, though, I'd like to present two highly respected models for understanding destructive behaviors and diagnosing roadblocks to communication. Similarly, we might see these problems as opportunities to acknowledge a problem and work together to fix it.

As you may recall, Julie and John Gottman's Four Horsemen of the Apocalypse are criticism, contempt, defensiveness, and stonewalling. The regular occurrence of these behaviors typically predicts failing, unhappy relationships. If you recognize these attitudes in your relationship, you might be more of a dick than you give yourself credit for. You're also likely headed for trouble.

Dicks are notoriously bad communicators in relationships. The Four Horsemen are rampant in their romantic lives. But we should also watch out for the Twelve Communication Roadblocks identified by Dr. Thomas Gordon, which he refers to as the "Dirty Dozen":

1. **Ordering, Directing:** "Stop feeling sorry for yourself . . ."

2. **Warning, Threatening:** "You'll never make friends if . . ." "I'm going to break up with you unless . . ."

3. **Moralizing, Preaching:** "If you would've only listened to me . . ." "You should just get over it . . ." "Patience is a virtue you clearly haven't learned . . ."

4. **Advising, Giving Solutions:** "What I would do is . . ." "You have to do it this way . . ."

5. **Persuading with Logic, Arguing:** "Here is why you're wrong . . ." "The facts are . . ." "Yes, but . . ."

6. **Judging, Criticizing, Blaming:** "You're not thinking maturely . . ." "That's just laziness . . ." "You started it . . ."

7. **Praising, Agreeing:** "Well, I think you're doing a great job!" "You're right—he sounds awful."

8. **Name-calling, Ridiculing:** "Crybaby." "That's stupid to worry about one low test grade."

9. **Analyzing, Diagnosing:** "What's wrong with you is . . ." "You seem grouchy." "I know you better than you know yourself . . ."

10. **Reassuring, Sympathizing:** "Don't worry." "You'll feel better." "Cheer up!"

11. **Questioning, Probing:** "Why did you do that?" "Who's calling you?" "What did you tell them?" "How come you looked at me that way?"

12. **Diverting, Sarcasm, Withdrawal:** "Let's talk about this later . . ." "Why don't you try running the world!?" Remaining silent, turning away

For the next exercise, look at the above behaviors and fill in your own. Becoming familiar with the ways your arguments break down into destructive fights characterized by retaliation and injury will allow you to catch this pattern early on and nip it in the bud. It's only through seeing these traps before you fall into them that you can make better choices about the direction to lead the conversation into so conflict becomes opportunity.

As you reflect upon and write responses to the query below, you install a pause button that gives you time between being scared, hurt, or angry, and doing something impulsive about those feelings. So please, take the thoughtfulness you use in this exercise with you as you go about your daily life.

Reflecting back on arguments that turned into fights, list up to five patterns you fall into that have negative consequences. For each one, provide up to three possible alternatives that might lead to mutually satisfying outcomes.

1. Pattern/Behavior

_____

_____

Alternative 1.

_____

_____

Alternative 2.

_____

_____

Alternative 3.

_____

_____

2. Pattern/Behavior

_____

_____

Alternative 1.

_____

_____

Alternative 2.

_____

_____

Alternative 3.

_____

_____

3. Pattern/Behavior

_____

_____

Alternative 1.

_____

_____

Alternative 2.

_____

_____

Alternative 3.

_____

_____

CHAPTER NINE

Don't Be a Dick to Yourself

In Meghan Doherty's book *How Not To Be a Dick: An Everyday Etiquette Guide*, she states that, "The first rule of not being a dick to others is: Don't be a dick to yourself."[37] Though I wouldn't make this my first rule, I agree that it's an important point to address.

Turning the tables on yourself by being self-critical, devaluing, or self-effacing doesn't help you avoid poor treatment from others. This is not a zero-sum game, as displacing our dickery onto ourselves only exacerbates the ill feelings that drive us to be dicks in the first place. We might think people will go easy on us if we bash ourselves—after all, aren't we already teaching ourselves a lesson? But no, others are more likely to jump in, labeling you negative, self-pitying, and miserable. These are not compliments. Yet self-criticism is a strategy many of us turn to. We have a whole arsenal of words, attitudes, and behavioral mechanisms to protect ourselves from others, but we don't use the same strategies to guard against self-harm.

Being a dick distracts us from our fear of vulnerability. As dicks, we cover up how terrified we are that others will reject us if they see our true selves. That way, when we're pummeled for being jerks, it's our *performance* that's yanked off the stage, not the real us.

The dramas in our lives that seem to necessitate dickish behavior are just distractions—and can be addictive. Dicks create crisis situations where there are none. Our authentic selves thus remain safely locked away, hidden by our performance of whatever crisis we come up with to throw others off our scent.

In her book *Codependent No More*,[38] Melody Beattie stresses this fact when she writes:

> *Strangely enough, problems can become addictive. If we live with enough misery, crisis and turmoil long enough, the fear and stimulation caused by problems can become a comfortable emotional experience . . . After a while, we can become so used to involving our emotions with problems and crisis that we may get and stay involved with problems that aren't our concern. We may even start making troubles or making troubles greater than they are to create stimulation for ourselves . . . When we're involved in a problem, we know we're alive. When the problem is solved, we may feel empty and void of feeling. Nothing to do. Being in a crisis becomes a comfortable place, and it saves is from our humdrum existence.*

We need to know how much stress we invite in our attempts to avoid a humdrum existence. Everyone in our emotional support network avoids us, leaving us in perpetual crisis, stewing in our own rationalized isolation. I diverge from Beattie, however, in my theory on the purpose of this action. She sees it as a means of "knowing we're alive," whereas I believe the crisis-driven dickery is a refuge from anxiety.

You're Being a Dick to Yourself When You Cause Burnout

It's amazing how much dickery results from unconscious invitations, one of which is, "I'm a doormat—walk all over me." This isn't our fate; we can work our way out of it. In allowing others to mistreat us, we're being dicks to ourselves, and worse, if having empathy means putting yourself in other people's shoes, then when we abuse ourselves we ask others to not only care about what we're going through, but to *feel* what we're experiencing too.

We wear people out when we incessantly put ourselves in situations that require them to ache with us. Sadly, it's only in such extreme contexts that many of us feel the care that others offer. Such a demand is not only taxing, though; it's a pretty dickish move. This is a form of self-harm as well, as such an extreme need for care requires that we chronically seek out problematic situations. Pain starts to feel like the only legitimate reason to request help from those around us. And if you've ever known someone who complained incessantly about a person hurting them, yet couldn't seem to break out of the abusive cycle, you know how much aggression and hostility it unleashes in them. This particular dickishness is divvied out to those in their support circles as well as to themselves.

My client Sandy is one of those people who wants everyone to notice her struggles, but has no sense of how it burdens those of us who care for her to walk through her troubles with her. For example, she informed me recently that her husband left her again, and she expected me to see only her victimization, dismissing the possibility that she had a role in the cycle she was describing.

"What happ—" I tried to say.

"Don't start, Dr. B. Just don't. You don't know what it's like to be lonely and depressed all the time. I have no one else. There's nothing to say."

"How many times has he done this?" I sighed.

"What?" Sandy said. "You don't remember? Don't I pay you enough to care about these things?"

"No amount of money could cover the cost of your exposure to Jerry's abuse. It hurts to empathize with you on this."

"My life hurts *you*?" Sandy was growing visibly indignant.

"You told yourself you'd never fall for Jerry's manipulations again. What happened?"

"You don't get what it's like to be alone!" she repeated.

If that were true, empathizing with Sandy wouldn't be so painful. Not understanding her anguish, I wouldn't have to hit pause and remind myself not to blame, criticize, or in any way sadden her. My role was to support her process of letting her guard down and encouraging the development of a sense of safety and security in our relationship. Yet there's no better lightning rod than a therapist for a dick who takes zero responsibility for what's wrong in his or her life.

"I get hurt by Jerry and everyone wants to blame me," Sandy groaned.

"If you're not receiving the response you're looking for, it's because you've told me many times you want out of your relationship with Jerry," I responded. "Getting riled up about how everyone 'blames you' for staying with Jerry actually gets in the way of realizing what a jerk he is. You dismiss the care and support in your life, and exhaust those people who love you the most. But worst of all, you're not doing the necessary emotional work."

When you're a dick to yourself, you expose yourself to "blaming the victim." It's tough, because being a dick is in fact a cry for help. Under compassionate conditions, heartbroken people receive due empathy. But a dick wields his or her victimization like a weapon against those who try to help, making care and compassion hard to access and sustain.

To Sandy, it seems like Jerry, her family, and her shrink are being dicks—yet maybe her mistreatment of herself, and the way she defends against help, is what needs an intervention.

When Sandy hit pause, having seen how hard it was for someone who cared about her to empathize with this, she finally asked herself some difficult questions.

"What am I getting from these outbursts? Is it possible I'm using Jerry's cruelty to place burdens on people?"

I knew what she was trying to communicate, then, and was able to reflect her feelings back at her in a way that didn't seem like an attack. This helped her experience her feelings rather than act them out in self-pitying ways that made it difficult to be around her, much less help.

"To be honest, I had no idea I was venting at you," Sandy exclaimed. "I was so hurt and scared, I couldn't see that *how* I was asking made it impossible for anyone to care—not *what* I was asking for."

Understanding Emotional Intoxication

A couple of decades into their marriage, Juan came home and announced to Mary that his doctor "found something unusual" during his yearly prostate examine. "They need to do some additional testing," Juan added. He had said this quite casually and was shocked when, after he'd settled into the couch and turned on the TV, he heard Mary weeping in the kitchen. A few days later they were still trying to get a handle on what happened in that moment. Since then they'd both seemed to open up in ways that were, as Juan put it, "unexpected."

"After so many years of *blah*," complained Mary, "I suddenly felt disoriented and lost. It wasn't just the fear of the, you know, the dreaded c-word. It was like being hit by a truck as I imagined what my life would be like without Juan."

"When Mary said that, I was hit by the feeling too," said Juan. "It was an all-consuming sense that this relationship mattered, but I didn't like it. That feeling made me uncomfortable. I told Mary she was being overly dramatic."

"Right," Mary said. "What started out as a tender, openhearted moment quickly became something else."

"We started acting like dicks," Juan said.

Deep, heartfelt emotions—what we all think we want in a relationship—open us up in surprising ways. Sometimes, even years into a relationship, profound emotions can sneak up, causing us to react, and act, in an unexpected fashion, including in ways that are directly opposed to how we really feel. Our awareness of the feelings we have for each other can be suppressed under years of mundane, shoulder-to-shoulder existence. When these feelings are unearthed then it shocks our system, causing us to feel exposed, unready to process the emotions we've longed for. It can both intimidate and intoxicate us. But acting out—the way we suppress our awareness of pain or fear—can also occur in response to vulnerability, especially when we feel insecure.

Social anxiety, especially toward people who've been important to us, sabotages our relationships by triggering confusing behavior that implies we don't care about those people. This makes it very difficult for others to accept us. And when they don't, that confirms the warped sense of "trust" we've developed—trust that others will inevitably reject us and so we need to protect ourselves. In this way, we inadvertently ward off that which we desire—love, care, intimacy, and the like. But sometimes, there's a glitch in the SNAFU system, and we "doth protest too much," to borrow Shakespeare's line about complaints that reveal the opposite to be true. Juan and Mary, in this sense, caught each other acting like dicks in their reactions to their care for each other and were able to pause long enough to question, "What is really going on here?"

"It was like all of our experiences together leading up to that point masked how I really felt about you," Mary said.

"When you wept, it jarred me," blurted Juan. "Seeing you so raw, so open, I once again realized how much I care about you, and how invested I am in this relationship. Which actually frightened me.

"My health scare passed, but the feeling of being cracked open didn't," Juan added. "I felt like that when we first met—like I wouldn't survive how much I cared about Mary. It felt like being stripped naked in public. Like looking at someone I believed I was thoroughly comfortable with, only to realize that that was a lie I told myself to avoid freaking out about how much I needed her."

"It happened to me too," Mary admitted. "The same old questions from my adolescence came flooding back, like does he really like me? Am I okay? Does he find me attractive? Can I trust him to stick around? It was torture."

"For me these felt like old unanswered questions," said Juan. "And they had lingered in my head since we first fell in love."

Our minds work hard to mitigate intoxicating emotions so we can function effectively. Like the liver, the mind's job is to help us detox—sober up emotionally, if you will—but for those of us whose formative years called for intense psychological defenses, the mind works *too* hard to protect us when we're adults.

"I woke up one day two decades into marriage with this man and it occurred to me he was a stranger. I thought, *I don't know him at all*, which freaked me out, so during the cancer scare, I shared that with him."

"I was crushed at first, because I didn't realize what Mary was getting at," Juan confided. "It hurt in a way I didn't even know I could be hurt anymore."

"I was shocked," admitted Mary.

"Me too," said Juan.

It's impossible to know what will break a defense system down, and there's no guarantee anything will. Maybe moments like the one Mary and Juan described are unusual cases. Regardless, when cracks in the system arise, they offer a window of opportunity to do things differently. Otherwise, your defenses will go back up in support of the status quo of coldness we and our partners will have silently resigned to.

During an opening, surviving the emotional intoxication is vital.

"The question of, *Where has he been all these years?* was replaced by, *Where have we been?*" said Mary.

Juan added, "Once we acknowledged how we *actually* feel about each other, and that I was still scared of losing her, it screwed me up in ways I could barely tolerate."

"Wanting you and needing you had become so foreign, when I felt some longing to be close to you again it was like being invaded by my own emotions."

"Now what?" Juan asked, desperately.

Emotional intoxication comes from accessing true but blocked feelings, and like other forms of intoxication, its intensity leads to hangovers. For this reason, many of us prefer to live in a gray world, where we blunt our emotions, or in full-on emotional abstinence. But we don't realize we're sharing this aloofness. It infects those around us.

"All I can say is, if we're going to survive these feelings, we need to do the therapy work together," Mary said.

The Easy Way Out Is Hard on Yourself

It's easy to feel blessed when life takes it easy on us. We may also avoid conflict to save ourselves from stress. But living a conflict-free life is a bad way to avoid being a dick. While you may not hurt yourself or anyone else, you won't truly be alive. Emotional investments put the heart at risk, but that's a life worth living. To not show up in matters of the heart due to terrified, conflicted emotions is to be a dick to yourself.

The opposite of dickery is not emotionally hollow, unprovocative, investment-free relationships. It wasn't for nothing that the mythical Greek king Agamemnon was willing to kill his daughter, Iphigenia, as part of the bargain he made with the gods to get his fleet to Troy. The goddess

Artemis demanded the human sacrifice. You may feel safe and neutral at sea—but inevitably you'll want to have something worth fighting for.

Take my client Josh, and his second wife, Madison. After sharing the extreme measures he took to curb anger toward their second child, Sophie, Josh mentioned how lucky they were that their first child, Elsa, was so easy. A "starter kid" was how he and Madison referred to her.

"Your marriage to your first wife, Shelly, was easy," I pointed out. "Was she your starter wife?"

"You know I was miserable," Josh said. "The once-a-week sex . . . It was awful *because* it was easy. We were *good enough* partners, but we didn't really challenge each other to be there for one another."

"You're kidding, right?" Madison exclaimed. "When we first met you seemed starved for some kind of actual connection. 'Not challenging each other' seems like a wild understatement, dear."

"Yes, you're right, I barely had to show up, emotionally. But that's not what I mean when I say Elsa was a starter kid," Josh said. "I most certainly am challenged to show up for her, and it blows my mind how much I love her. Sometimes I just feel like I'm just not going to make it when it comes to her sister. Sophie requires so much more of my patience and tolerance and compassion than Elsa did."

Josh was absent in his first marriage—and his first wife Shelly didn't show up either. There is no worse fate than emotional isolation. Feeling romantically stifled, cut off from your partner's sincerest emotions, truly hurts. In relationship doldrums, we both crave and unconsciously defend against intimacy, empathy, and emotional investment. We've essentially given up. And if that state feels safe, it's only because we've put ourselves in solitary confinement, where we remain stuck. Josh broke out when he met Madison, who required that he show up not only for her as a partner and husband, but also for their children.

"If you were in the same state with your kids that you were with Shelly, all this anger and frustration wouldn't be happening," I told him.

"I know," Josh said. "Sophie is just such a tough kid."

"Like you were?"

"Exactly," Josh said. "I love how—unlike with Elsa—I'm Sophie's go-to. I never imagined after Elsa that I could be a kid's first choice. It's just that Sophie keeps getting busted. Her kindergarten teacher has a 'talk' with me every other day, and at this point I feel like I'm the one in trouble. She got kicked out of ballet. Now, the other parents scowl at me when I pick her up."

"That sounds stressful."

"It is! I ask her, 'Sophie, why won't you behave? Sophie, what's wrong?' Her answer is always 'I don't know, Dad,' with that twinkle in her eye. So yeah, she's a chip off the old block. But there are times when it takes every ounce of restraint in me not to blow up at her!"

So, was the docile nature of his "starter kid," Elsa, really such a blessing? Maybe. Josh and Madison love her dearly, and she's an excellent sister to Sophie. But Elsa didn't prepare Josh for a five-year-old who acts the way five-year-olds often act. He had to develop ways to hit pause and resist dickery to, as he put it, "survive Sophie."

Inviting in and surviving a more active love requires you to navigate through, not around, the treacherous twists and turns on the road to a happy destiny. Being involved with people, and life in general, means swinging at curve balls, not dropping the bat and quitting when things get hard. So, while softer, easier relationships may come around, they aren't necessarily *better*, as they don't prepare us for the drama we need to negotiate as we pursue healthy, rewarding lives in which we're not dicks.

EXERCISE: DICK-TO-SELF

This exercise's goal is to identify the overt or covert ways in which you act like a dick to yourself and inadvertently trigger counterattacks from others. Dick-to-self behaviors work to:

- Defend you from feeling vulnerable

- Suppress your anxiety related to escalating attachment and trust

- Protect you from intoxicatingly intense emotions when your heart is at risk

- Push others away by acting out emotions that feel intolerable

The following table provides examples of dick-to-self behaviors, how they play out in relationships, and the impact these behaviors have on relationships. It's followed by questions to help you isolate dickish characteristics in your relationships.

Dick-to-Self Behavior	How It Plays Out In Your Relationships	The Impact on These Relationships
Example A: Intense financial management that results in unnecessary stress and a sense of victimization.	My obsession with money leads me to micro-manage our finances and criticize my family for spending that I deem unnecessary.	I control our finances, but also resent this burden. My wife feels left out, and as if I don't trust her.
Example B: I forgive my partner's destructive behaviors and excuse them when others question my passivity.	I act as if I'm okay with people treating me badly, and find ways to ignore advice and distance myself from those who want to help.	I feel disconnected from my partner and a coldness from everyone else.
Example C: I stress out over the discrepancy I see between how kind the people in my life are toward others, and how cold, selfish, and withholding they seem toward me.	I pretend I'm unaffected, but then freeze others out when they need something from me.	I've built a tolerance for relatively unacceptable behavior from myself and others.

Do any of these examples resonate with you? What is it about them that seems familiar? Now ask yourself:

- Do you see ways that being a dick to yourself manifests in relationships?

- Do the ways you treat yourself invite others to avoid or mistreat you?

- What happens when you feel mistreated and *don't* act it out (that is, don't withhold or react aggressively)?

- What is it like to sit with those feelings?

- What is it like to share them with someone you believe is interested and cares (or to at least imagine doing so)?

CHAPTER TEN

Checkmate on Dickery

This chapter is heavily influenced by the twelve-step motto, "instincts on rampage balk at investigation." We often resist seeing the deep-seated truths that our bad behaviors express, and when asked to consider how we're being dicks, our defensive, knee-jerk reactions make us look even worse. For this reason, the Twelve Steps include the inventory: a self-assessment to acknowledge our personal assets and deficits. It's only through honest appraisal that we see how we contribute to problems and conflicts. And awareness empowers us to change.

At first, many react to the inventory the way a hand responds to a hot flame; we recoil at the notion of surveying our behavior. The tendency is to equate self-inventory with accepting blame or practicing self-criticism. However, as they say in the business world, "not all inventories are written in red ink." While assessing your flaws, account for your positive qualities as well. When it comes to a personal inventory, gifts, talents, and skills are just as valid as shortcomings.

Focusing on yourself can feel like going back to the scene of a crime, except not only are you the perpetrator, you're the lead prosecutor. Some of us prefer to remain innocent until proven guilty—and deny everything. That sounds safer, but as we've learned, the cost of denial is too high. Rejecting responsibility for our actions locks us into our dickish moods and justifications for behaviors that put us in harm's way. Ultimately, we become hardened in the belief that the world is out to get us, and isolate from others, including those who offer love, care, and support. To skip the personal inventory is to accept *anxious apartness*, a.k.a. loneliness.

Avoiding accountability for problems, issues, or conflicts in relationship provides serious cover for the sneak-attack that is isolation. Many of us feel a mind-boggling loneliness in bed with our long-term partner, the kind of quiet desperation that comes from fearing an invisible enemy who operates through guerilla warfare—shots fired at any given time or place, without warning, and from long range or point blank. These are the most fatal shots for relationships—and they derive from our unwillingness to leave our camouflaged position and take responsibility for our actions.

When done in tandem, the personal inventory and the accountability it creates allow for a safe space to drop the dickish attitude and codevelop ideas to promote intimacy and empathy. It's like a cease-fire that's followed by a peace treaty to end the war of isolation and loneliness.

I received an email that demonstrates this phenomenon from a client I worked with before and after she went to rehab. In her words:

> When I got home from rehab, I was beyond unpleasant. That wasn't so unusual given what my behavior was like before. But I thought I'd gotten better, so this was disappointing. What was really shocking though was that Jim was acting like a jerk, too.
>
> I think I'd been feeling put upon because Jim kept reminding me of what great lengths he'd gone to care for me and the kids as I was bottoming out from alcohol. I got so sick of it. I mean, sure I was thankful, but his constant fishing for praise made it hard for me to take a breath and ask myself how I felt about where I was, and what I'd been through, and where I'm headed to now as a wife and mother. Eventually it felt like he was guilt-tripping me, and meanwhile he thought I seemed ungrateful. We both felt unheard, and even after all we'd been through, we questioned whether we could accept each other warts and all.
>
> We'd never faced that question before. I'd been drunk for most of the last three years of our relationship, but ironically the question of whether we could stay together in my sobriety was among the biggest challenges we ever faced.

So I asked Jim to try the inventory thing, explaining that we would put our judgments down and talk about our roles in everything that was going on. We agreed to keep the focus on ourselves, like you said, and do a thorough review of our actions so we don't leave anything out that might be in each other's lists.

It was hard at first—scarier than the thought of losing him—but when I analyzed how crazy I'd acted since rehab, I had to admit to Jim that I was worried he'd stop loving me if I got well. Deep down, I dreaded that Jim only loved saving me. The fear was that by getting sober, I took away his role as the knight in shining armor, which seemed to bring him validation.

I'm sobbing by the time I get through telling Jim this. Then when I looked up, he was crying too. When it was Jim's turn to do an inventory, he admitted to fearing that I could only love him in that knight's role, and now that I was better, I'd find someone I didn't associate with all the difficulties we'd gone through.

Okay with Being Okay

What this looks like well into recovery, of course, looks dramatically different. One day my client Anne asked, "What do I do now?" She'd been in substance abuse recovery for over ten years, she maintained a long-term abstinence from sexually compulsive behavior, and had worked through her caregiving addiction after divorcing her second husband. Both of her exes were raging dicks, but she had remarried a kind, generous man who reciprocated her love.

"You mean now that you're no longer at war with the world?" I asked.

"Yeah," replied Anne. "Now that I've learned to hit pause and feel raw and vulnerable with a man who loves the real me."

We live in a culture that pathologizes us for feeling vulnerable. It disparages sincerity. Openheartedness and other forms of sensitivity are viewed as signs of weakness. And as a result, we don't know how to live comfortably in emotional experiences. Feeling strongly about another person is crazy-making; we're not geared to make sense of what's going on in our hearts and minds, and all we want to do is get out of that state of feeling threatened in our own skin.

"What's wrong with me, Dr. Borg?" asked Anne. "After all the work I've done to stop getting involved with basket-case men, why am I freaking out at getting what I've been saying I wanted for years?"

"It's probably time to learn to be okay with being okay," I said.

Sometimes we have to question whether the work that we do is about self-improvement, as we tend to believe, or rather self-acceptance. As long as we're trying fix someone else's difficulties, we cannot get a handle on our own, but eventually the time comes to get good with ourselves. Other people's problems have operated as a distraction from what we've yet to accept about ourselves. But a personal inventory of our part in problematic relationships will make hiding these tendencies difficult at best.

"You've side-stepped the issue of self-acceptance again and again by getting caught up in what's wrong with whatever dude has taken center stage in your life," I said.

Anne grew up in a devoutly Catholic Italian-American household. Her father, a hardworking "tunnel rat," worked in the New York City subway system. Her mother was a school teacher. They loved Anne and her sister, and for the most part they loved each other. But Anne's parents were unable to express this love directly, and by the time Anne was a teenager, she had begun attracting older men who were physically and sexually abusive. The dangerous relationship dynamic decreased as she got older, yet rather than disappearing completely, it persisted in the cold and cruel treatment she suffered at the hands of her first two husbands, as well as several of the men she dated after she began therapy with me.

Anne believed she had grown up in a loving home and could not figure out why she kept replaying toxic relationships with men. However, upon analysis, and unbeknownst to Anne when she first began therapy, her parent's inability to express their affection for her was interpreted as apathy and she wound up internalizing this suspicion as a statement of her worth. Combined with the abusive men she encountered in her adolescence was a history of drug and alcohol abuse, several police incidents, and despite an above-average intelligence, poor academic performances.

"I was crying out for help," Anne said one day in therapy. "Each bad boyfriend, each call from a teacher, or police officer, or friend's parent was met with a freaked-out paralysis by my parents. There was nothing that could happen that would make them be proactive. At least that's how it felt."

I wouldn't say there's no such thing as self-love; I would say, though, that the adult expression of self-love takes the form of relationships we invite into our lives. When we welcome dicks into our lives (or anyone who becomes some kind of distraction against knowing and accepting ourselves as we are), we make it difficult to see who we are, what we need, and what we want, especially in romantic relationships.

"I just gave up on getting anything and everything that I ever wanted or needed, especially from another person," Anne said.

Being with dicks also justifies keeping our defenses up, making the process of self-inventory questionable at best.

"Therapy shifted things for me," Anne said. "When I took an honest look at my old version of events, it began to feel incompatible with what I was seeing now. I had taken the way my parents treated me in my childhood so personally. What else could I do? Then I carried those horrible feelings into all my relationships. And each one confirmed the horrible thoughts I had about myself."

The last thing Anne's parents meant to do was neglect her and give her the impression that she had no value to them. But their own lives—busy lives full of personal, professional, and familial stressors—made reassuring Anne impossible in the ways she needed. Anne blamed herself for this, as neglected children often do, and recreated scenario after scenario in which her limited value was confirmed by the men she chose to be with.

It's only when we put our defenses down that we're able to take inventory to see others and ourselves as we truly are. And only with such awareness that we can realistically accept both ourselves and others. Anne saw herself as a person with limited, if any, value. She worked hard in therapy to confront, challenge, and let go of this sentiment. Nonetheless, accepting the love of her third husband required confronting that old image of herself that had tormented her for so long. Accepting this new image and her own lovability was a profound, anxiety-provoking challenge.

"Funny," sighed Anne. "I guess now I'm the basket case."

"Nope," I retorted. "You're just in a new relationship and affected by the experience of taking a real risk with someone who is beginning to matter."

Navigating the Insecurity of Accepting the World As Is

Several years ago, it was popular in twelve-step circles for people to blurt out, "It's not *going to* be okay—*it already is.*"

As I said in the beginning of this book, the message of all the world's mystics regardless of religious or spiritual bent is that *everything is okay.* Perhaps we need not leave this outlook in the metaphysical realm and can consider it a way of experiencing the world when there is a balance between how we feel, act, and are responded to. You might say that being okay is a state of harmony between these aspects, which might explain why it's so elusive. Instead of accepting that we're already okay, we tend to make this a goal for some uncertain future.

After my client Doug received news that he and his husband Gerard had been approved to adopt an infant daughter, he started analyzing his marriage in this way. All the turmoil they had gone through acting out and mistreating each other was really a refusal to accept that everything was okay. Or as Gerard put it: "From when gay marriage was approved to the green lights each step of the way in the adoption process, every time things worked out in our favor, the relationship got worse."

Why is it so hard to accept that we're okay? Well, when we defend ourselves from the anxiety that comes with being close to someone, refusing to believe we'll be unharmed by them, eventually even feeling safe in a relationship is hard. Most of us have no real sense of how much risk our emotional investments place us in. And though we have a whole psychological defense system designed to limit our awareness of this risk, there are times when our vulnerability can no longer be suppressed. To feel okay is to be aware of how much we cherish the relationships that allow us to feel like ourselves.

After this period of pain and disruption in their marriage, I asked Doug and Gerard to summarize what they'd taken from the experience.

"Could it be that caring about each other, and everything we'd built so far, felt so intense that all we could do to maintain our sanity was try to kill it?" Doug asked.

"*Try* to kill it is an understatement," mused Gerard.

"I just couldn't believe things were working out in our favor," admitted Doug. "I thought I was helping, but I'm sure it felt more like meddling or sabotage than like actual help. I just had to mess with the process."

"I was embarrassed," said Gerard. "I couldn't stand it that things were working out and I blamed you for that anxiety. I couldn't be honest about how terrified I was that my wish to have a family was finally coming true. It was too much. Sometimes I really hated you."

"I felt that," said Doug. "Every hoop we squeezed through to get closer to our dreams also made us targets for people who would not accept us."

"Yes," agreed Gerard, "people like us."

"Amazing what little trouble I had protecting myself against the ways the world seemed to be against me, against us," Doug said. "But when all the lights were green, I realized it was me who couldn't accept me, us, or our circumstance as we—as they—were."

"I must have felt the same because even though I was the one really pushing to make this happen, I joined you in the bad behavior that kept screaming: *You two have made a huge f—king mistake by going for it.*"

"Risky stuff, trying to make all that happen," Doug acknowledged.

"Accepting the hand life dealt us?" Gerard said.

"No, no—are you high? This was *not* supposed to happen," Doug said. "There's no way I actually thought we'd pull this off. I'm not sure when, if ever, I'm going to accept this."

"Because it's scary as hell?"

"Yeah, thanks for rubbing that in."

Why We Can't Just Keep to Our Side of the Street

Not everyone has an addiction, compulsion, or "allergy" to a substance or habit that introduces them to the Twelve Steps. But all can benefit from recovery lessons, so I'll provide an overview of the steps I find most helpful in letting go of dickery, as well as a process to abstain from being a dick.

In the twelve-step model, taking inventory is how one learns about, accepts, and eventually corrects so-called "character defects." It's Step Four: *Made a searching and fearless moral inventory of ourselves.* Think of it as an account of what needs cleaning up. Steps Five through Nine involve acting on that awareness. We hold ourselves responsible for past behaviors, as well as what drives and sustains them, and attain the will to remove these character defects while we make amends with those we've injured.

When this is all done, we reach what's known in twelve-step jargon as the "keeping our side of the street clean" step. *Continued to take personal inventory and when we were wrong promptly admitted it,* Step Ten, is most pertinent to our exploration. Also known as the "maintenance step," it offers the recovering person an opportunity to put the awareness earned through inventory to use in daily life. Taking personal inventory and promptly admitting your wrongs is the golden rule to resist behavioral rationalizations that lead to dickery. This takes the accountability for our dickery fully off others, allowing us to see and break down the logic we've used to justify our stance toward others.

"No inventory taking" is jargon in the twelve-step community for sparing our partner from our judgments and criticism. The saying is a way to remind ourselves to not be dicks, which sometimes feels like an impossible task. I've found, though, that the best prevention against taking someone else's inventory—your husband's, your wife's, your partner's, your colleague's, your pal's—is (drum roll, please) *taking your own.*

Putting Yourself in a Position to be Hurt

Jeff was newly sober and complained bitterly about a boss who had miraculously not fired him for his unexplained absences, misuse of company funds, and defiant behavior during the extreme drinking and drug abuse that led to his bottom. His boss was a recovering alcoholic who understood addiction and believed that with patience and tolerance he could help when Jeff hit bottom. I listened to Jeff's tirade, then asked, "What about you? How do you contribute to the problems between you and your boss?"

"What?" Jeff exclaimed in what sounded like righteous indignation.

Behaving like a dick always boomerangs right back, and Jeff's difficulty accepting his boss's tolerance and generosity was causing him more problems than his alcoholism. His boss understood the nature of alcohol-fueled assholery, but had a harder time being compassionate toward Jeff in his newly sober ingratitude.

In recovery, resentment is considered the most toxic emotion since it places us in a position to be hurt. Our resentment may offer an instant jolt of relief in the form of anger, but the blame is focused on an external target, and if we don't account for our part in the situation, others will continue to protect themselves from us, leaving us alone in an intolerable state.

In Jeff's case, he can't get a handle on why the people he hurt have neither forgiven nor forgotten his destructive actions, despite the fact that he is now sober. The returns on his "purposeful forgetting" will diminish over time, however, so he has to make a deliberate effort to make things right.

Jeff, in his role as the garden-variety dick, felt consistently tempted to project his faults onto someone else, preferably someone near and dear who *really* needed an inventory.[39] "After all," he asked his boss, "didn't you help me get sober to help yourself? Isn't that what you twelve-step people do? Seems kind of self-serving, yeah?"

Jeff's boss wasn't buying Jeff's attempts to celebrate himself for his grand accomplishment. Though relieved and supportive of Jeff's recovery, he didn't see sobriety as an excuse to continue rude, destructive behavior. "It's what we do, Jeff. We help people who express a desire to be helped. But we don't accept them stomping all over us and taking advantage of our generosity."

"Aren't I helping you by letting you help me?"

"Jeff, please. You're acting like a jerk, and alcohol is no longer an excuse."

"I know that. I've sobered up, thank you very much. It's your expectations that are stressing me out."

It sucks to accept our character defects and absorb feelings we've long tried to diminish. But so long as we see our flaws in others, and misperceive counterattacks as unprovoked attacks, we will remain isolated, at war with the world.

"That may be so, Jeff," said his boss. "But now we have to figure out if your bad attitude is just a last vestige of your active addiction, or who you *really* are."

"I don't know if I can do this," Jeff admitted.

"No one does."

Intervening with your obsessions, compulsions, and character defects is also referred to as "cleaning house." And in recovery, some identify the moment of honesty and discovery that comes afterward as "the end of isolation." By putting our *seemingly* defensive, but ultimately *offensive* weapons down, we embrace the risk that others will accept us as we are, vulnerable and pained. We finally use authentic emotions to connect with others. Being honest and open about who we are, that willingness to share, is how we accept ourselves and others.

It was easy to rationalize our behaviors without a witness to help us off the ledge of self-deception. We used to tell ourselves, *I'm not a dick—they are*, clutching this survival mechanism if only because no one was looking.

Mapping Out Your Positive Attributes

Because we've been so averse to accepting others, ourselves, and the world as they are, it can take a couple passes at the inventory for us to realize how wonderful various aspects of our life may be. Our psychological defenses didn't allow anything in, not the good, the bad, or anything in between. We were so busy protecting ourselves, we couldn't discern friend from foe. And so often the surprise effect of an inventory is that we see ourselves as lovable.

This first glimpse has far-reaching possibilities. Being loved by someone else may be an entryway to loving ourselves. The inventory isn't meant to strip us down and shame us for our dickery, but to open the door to a realm where we discover things about ourselves, our history, and the world around us that merit acceptance.

A powerful form of self-care, inventory asks you to look in the mirror, see how the pluses mitigate the minuses, and weigh for yourself the net results. Traits that you like or even love about yourself will help you recover from the things you dislike, hate, or feel embarrassed or ashamed about. That's what I mean when I say this is an inside job.

Regular inventories result in being "right-sized"—practicing humility as a daily endeavor. You go about life recognizing that you're neither better nor worse than others, interacting with people eye-to-eye as equals.

When all's said and done, inventory is a wonderful thing. But to get that sense of balance, let's counter what may seem like the negative side of self-reflection by mapping out the positives. Often with chronic dicks, the non-red ink part of the inventory—what I'm calling *asset mapping*—turns out to be more difficult than the "here's what an asshole I am" part. And why is that? Our good qualities have caused many of us to be exploited, attacked, and envied in our past.

Some people don't realize that envy is intolerable to receive as well. Unlike jealousy, a temporary emotion that blends desire with possessiveness, as in "I want what you got," or "Don't take what's mine," envy is a lasting bitterness in which we feel contempt over an unattainable desire and would just as soon destroy its source. Envy can also complicate our feelings about our own strengths and virtues, since our enviable qualities may have been exploited by some and resented by others in the past. Sometimes, being a dick provides a shelter from having to acknowledge our qualities and the complicated, hostile reactions they occasionally engender.

I had a client named Nicolás who was a womanizer *par excellence*. Good-looking, funny, and smart, he was an actor and bartender whose greatest turn on was emotionally unavailable women. The more rejected he felt, the longer his interest endured. If the unattainable woman was finally ensnared by his charm, he would then believe it was "different this time," and he could change a partner's emotionally distant ways. It would all come crashing down, of course. Almost every time, once the woman showed up emotionally, convinced by Nicolás's obsessive efforts, he'd ghost her.

No one was more convinced than Nicolás that he was an incurable dick. He had no trouble criticizing himself, feeling remorse, diminishing his virtues, and self-diagnosing as a "narcissist and maybe even a sociopath." At times he rampaged against himself. And I couldn't argue against what his acting-out behavior confirmed. But I also believed Nicolás's history told a more complicated story.

When Nicolás was five-years-old, his mother claimed that his father was unfaithful. It turned out, however, that Nicolás's mother was the one who had an affair. She pushed his father away, and his dad moved out and took Nicolás's older brother with him, leaving Nicolás to manage his mother's misery himself. From that point on, Nicolás became his mom's "Little Man." As her caretaker, he put every virtue he possessed to service for his "sad mommy."

Underneath Nicolás's dickish behavior as an adult, he remained the dutiful caretaker he was as a kid. He ran through numerous women's lives appearing to be the perfect partner, yet after a few sexual encounters he would disappear. Once in a while, this routine would hit a snag; he'd find a woman in deep emotional trouble and throw himself into her care. Inevitably, though, the relationship would fall apart and Nicolás would return to meaningless sexcapades fueled by indignation and righteousness.

"See! I'm a really bad guy," he would say. "I'd be better off accepting that and acting accordingly."

At first, Nicolás found it hard to believe I didn't agree with his devastating assessment of himself. I refused to see him simply as a narcissist who should accept his fate and banish himself to the realm of the unlovable. I suggested Nicolás take an inventory of his behavior to acknowledge and address whatever drove his dickery. There, he discovered a lost, lonely child who no amount of acting out—using and abusing women—could get rid of.

In inventory, acknowledging the ways he'd been a "bad guy," a "user," or "a prick" was easy for Nicolás. The challenge was to accept himself as a loving and loveable person who was simply terrified to allow himself to be exposed to the overwhelming needs of others again.

Nicolás developed his pattern of dickery to hide his good qualities, to throw women off his track. But in the process, he hid these qualities from himself. It took a long time, and a lot of bruises—including a punch delivered by a woman he brought for an unannounced session of couple's therapy with me—for Nicolás to finally see his good side. He acknowledged his fear that, "If anyone saw my kindness, I'd be right back in that boat I was in with my mom when my dad left."

It will be a lifelong process for Nicolás to accept his non-dick status and trust that he will not be exploited for doing so. But Nicolás is committed to the inventory work he began with me, and occasionally he checks in to let me know he's still allowing himself to love and be loved.

By All Means, Judge Each Other

Dick or not, we've all got built-in defense systems that take qualities we dislike in ourselves and, rather than deal with them, allow us to perceive those intolerable things in others. Colloquially, we call this *projecting*. We walk around in this state of anarchy every day, imposing the bitterness, hatred, and self-pity in us on others, ignoring hurt, sadness, and fear simmering in our minds. These unacknowledged, unaddressed, unshared, and *uncontained* feelings grow from molehills to mountains when left to pile up inside us. Still, we're terrified that these emotions say something more than that we're merely human.

We're geared to adjust to difficult circumstances. Like a strange emotional superpower, we can take trauma and heartbreak, and construe that pain as others' shortcomings rather than absorb its full burden of anger and self-loathing. It's human nature, then, to judge one another. But if we recognize that these attitudes are just as much reflections of ourselves—our own failures and flaws—we ready ourselves for a healing mix of compassion and empathy. So, go right ahead. Judge away. Judge to your heart's content, till the cows come home, until you're all judged out, and can judge no more. But do so in love.

EXERCISE: ADDRESSING ROADBLOCKS TO INVENTORY

Taking inventory is less about our overt behavior and more about what it covers up. Because our deep fear of vulnerability has been blocked from our awareness, most of us have not considered, much less shared, what's behind our dickery. So let's hit pause, reflect, and write down the attitudes and behaviors that acted as roadblocks to this sort of personal inventory.

Think of a recent time when you were a dick to someone important in your life—a romantic partner, colleague, family member, or friend. Write down your immediate reflections and feelings regarding *your* part (and only your part) in the incident:

_____

_____

_____

_____

_____

_____

_____

Now without overthinking it, answer the following questions:

- What are your initial thoughts about what you wrote?

- How has identifying, reflecting upon, and writing about your part in the problem changed your perspective? Looking at the bigger picture, is the problem is acute or ongoing? And if so, do you have any idea why?

- Are you concerned that taking responsibility for past actions could damage significant relationships in your life? Has this happened before? Have there been threats to end relationships when you've admitted fault?

EXERCISE: POSITIVE MEMORIES MAKE STRONG FOUNDATIONS

Having behaved like dicks makes it obvious what was wrong with a relationship, and who bears responsibility for its failings. But few of us were always like that. Think back on your relationship with the person involved in the incident reflected on in the Roadblocks to Inventory exercise. Was there a time when you both felt more positive about one another? Remember the time before the negative experiences started to build up: a particular occasion when you did something together that went well and you enjoyed being together, a warm, connected feeling. This could be an experience had while traveling, an important life event, a tender romantic memory, or a time spent doing a favorite activity at home.

Now take a few minutes and come up with your version of that story, your part in what was good about it, with the goal to remember and visualize the experience as vividly as possible, focusing on warm, loving feelings, gratitude, appreciation, and so on. Next, write down the three most positive aspects of the experience.

1. _____

_____

_____

2. _____

_____

_____

3. _____

_____

_____

EXERCISE: AFFIRMATIONS

Let's consider the many positive qualities you possess. We're putting this up against your history of dickery, so let us be generous as we recognize ways in which you're loving, caring, trustworthy, and even loveable.

Example:

I have a good sense of humor.

1. I _____

_____

_____

_____

2. I _____

_____

_____

_____

3. I _____

_____

_____

_____

_____

Note the difference in how you see and feel about yourself when inventory is done in red ink—the standard inventory you've done all along by believing you were terrible—versus how you think of yourself after an inventory in black ink. Asset mapping balances you out. Spend some time jotting down thoughts on how you can maintain this feeling:

_____

_____

_____

_____

_____

EXERCISE: ASSET MAPPING

Now that we have a sense of what our assets are, let's put some of these attributes up against broad brush strokes of dickery in your past to see how the assets can better impact your relationships. As you know, being a dick can sneakily affect mundane, everyday activities.

In the left column, record your strengths; in the right, areas that still need improving. In each case, pause to consider the balance of these assets and deficits to gauge how you may use your resources to work through and let go of the defensive dickery.

Capacities, Gifts, and Skills

What are the key attributes I bring to relationships? In what ways have I used these capacities to be a better partner?	How have I underutilized these capacities, gifts, and skills? What seems to be the outcome?
Asset:	Deficit:
How might utilizing these *attributes* mitigate the effects of the deficit if we work together with honesty and willingness?	

Commitment

How have I taken responsibility for my part in each crisis, conflict, problem, or issue in this relationship?	How have I avoided accountability?
Asset:	Deficit:

How might utilizing this *commitment* asset mitigate the effects of the deficit if we work together with honesty and willingness?

Authenticity

In what ways have I been authentic—as in open, accurate, and honest—with people in my life?	In what ways have I been inauthentic—denying feelings and thoughts, minimizing problems and behaviors—and thus avoided being intimate with others?
Asset:	Deficit:
How might this *authenticity* asset mitigate the effects of my deficit?	

Alliance

How have I been available to others, built alliances, and sought to share with others to experience intimate connections?	How have I isolated from others and avoided the possibility of intimate, empathetic connections?
Asset:	Deficit:

How might this *alliance* asset mitigate the effects of my deficit?

Meeting Needs

In what ways do I let myself be nurtured? How do I contribute to my own health and well-being? Am I willing to accept help?	How am I unwilling to receive help from others? How do I avoid support for my health and well-being? Do I fail to care for myself?
Asset:	Deficit:

How might this *need-meeting* asset mitigate the effects of my deficit?

Decision-Making

What healthy choices have I made?	When have I avoided making choices?
Asset:	Deficit:

How might this *decision-making* asset mitigate the effects of my deficit?

Emotional Openness

How and when am I able to share my feelings with others?	What kinds of things block me from sharing feelings?
Asset:	Deficit:

How might utilizing this *emotional-openness* asset mitigate the effects of the deficit if we work together with honesty and willingness?

Following Through

What resources allow me to resolve unfinished business and follow through on commitments I've made?	What interferes with my ability to resolve unfinished business and follow through on commitments?
Asset:	Deficit:
How might this *following-through* asset mitigate the effects of my deficit?	

Now, answer the following questions:

- Do you overemphasize your faults, or is your inventory accurate?

- If you focus too much on negative experiences, write down some examples of positive experience you've had in the past few weeks.

- Observe your self-talk. Consider ways to change negative self-talk into something positive that is still believable.

- When you notice yourself drifting into negative thoughts, ask if they really make sense. What happens when you challenge those thoughts? Can you find better ways to look at situations and people?

PART IV

DICKS

IN

RECOVERY

CHAPTER ELEVEN

Meeting Manipulators with Compassion

It's time to flip the script and show dickish manipulators compassion and understanding. Having strong mental health means being able to pause between thoughts and actions. The pause allows the dick in your life— whether that's you or someone else—to create a space with more options for more acceptable behavior. With this space, the dick can recognize triggered reactions and nip them in the bud. In a work environment, this ability can result in team-building, a deeper understanding of each team member's assets and deficits, and improved productivity. What's more, when rhetorical traps are spotted before falling into them, the dick can make better choices about what direction to take a conversation to avoid conflict.

The Pause That Can Save Any Relationship

My client Austin offers an example of how much better you can feel when you pause before acting or speaking. His dickery went back fifteen years, but once its dynamics became clear, he found a new way of relating to others. No matter how entrenched our roles seem, there is always another way forward.

"After my parents split up, I didn't feel welcome in my dad's life," Austin said. He had just returned from his father's funeral. "His new wife and I never got along. The problem, as I saw it, was my stepmother's lack of hospitility."

"Hospit*ility*?" I said.

"Sorry, I meant *hospitality*. But there was *hostility* in it. I spent years hiding my resentment with a superficial civility, believing that I was being generous by attempting to accept my dad's new life at all."

Generosity and aggression are strange bedfellows. Built-up resentment from bending over backwards to meet someone else's expectations actually contorts the mind. Our behaviors, actions, and attitudes take strange positions.

Austin was fifteen when his dad left his mom to marry Suzanne. The break-up felt like a betrayal for Austin and his younger sister. But even more painful was the realization that in order to maintain a relationship with their once idealized father, the kids had to accept his new wife as a member of the family. Austin and his sister were unrealistically expected to treat Suzanne with hospitality. They couldn't do it. So, while Suzanne's "hospitility" was being unearthed, so was Austin's.

"We had a stupid disagreement after the funeral about items that were personal to me—photos I'd sent to my dad of my son. I wanted them back. Suzanne said no, but I took them anyway without telling her. Then on the way to the airport she called enraged, saying, 'You took the only pictures I have of my grandson.' I was about to defend myself, but instead I hit pause. I hung up. I was so relieved! At that moment, our relationship was over.

"And yet," Austin said, sighing, "something started to gnaw at me. It was anxiety, which led to sadness, and a sense of loss. *What was going on?* I wondered. Why had I not seen that Suzanne had genuine feelings for me and my wife and kid? My bitterness over my father's manipulative demands blinded me to what was going on. I never realized I was placing the same type of demands upon my family, who wound up loving Suzanne as a grandmother and mother-in-law despite the inauthentic way I did.

"Was I scapegoating Suzanne for my father's behavior? Was I blaming her for my own bad attitude? I started to think I'd inherited my dad's manipulative behavior and Suzanne was merely an innocent bystander. It felt like I was being strangled by my feelings, choking on a resentment that I'd meant to use to crush my family's feelings for my stepmother."

Believing it was charitable simply to tolerate Suzanne, Austin had displaced decades' worth of anger and resentment onto her in order to convince himself that his dad's selfish behavior was acceptable. The *hospitility* Austin showered upon Suzanne was a symptom of unaddressed betrayal. Expressing his true feelings about his father breaking up the family would have been too costly, so Austin developed elaborate routines fraught with dickery to keep the anxiety about losing his dad at bay.

But after the funeral, something shifted.

"I called Suzanne and apologized. She accepted. I offered to send the pictures back, but also to send more. It felt like being freed after a long prison sentence. Yes, it's true, it was my father's fault, but until then I'd been committed to maintaining the lie that she deserved all the blame."

Can Your Business Survive the Dick in Its Midst—Even if That's You?

You might not want to build up your psychological defenses to tolerate workplaces run by bullies, paranoids, and emotional manipulators. But seeing these behaviors as reactions to organizational threats can allow you to respond with compassion and understanding, resulting in solid trust and team-building. With that in mind, might it serve you to work through what may seem like unbearable interpersonal circumstances rather than torpedo a project and jump ship?

When conflicts arise at work, I suggest each party examine what he or she did and its effect on the rest of the team. When we agree to regular "spot-check inventories" of what's going on, not only do we pause and assess rather than scapegoat or deflect, we feel encouraged to show awareness of others' feelings afterward in anticipation of future inventories. This agreement creates a safe space to keep the focus on oneself—*I honestly assess mine, you honestly assess yours, and we recognize our faults, together.*

Taking stock helps to register anxiety and process feelings together rather than act on that anxiety in a way that confirms each other's suspicions. Reflection and discussion is always better than judgment, cross-talking, and criticism, no matter how cathartic the latter sounds. The effectiveness of this technique lies in each party feeling safe to say what is needed without unwelcome feedback or defensiveness. Listening respectfully, each party learns from *and* about the other. With practice, they become increasingly able to lay aside criticism and get back to work.

My client Owen was a founding partner of a boutique consulting firm where, from his point of view, management had lost sight of the core vision and goal. Organizational psychologists call this "reason for being" the institution's *primary task*. Owen frantically told me that though he needed to confront the company's "identity crisis," he had to do so in way that was constructive despite being "pissed off."

Owen invited me to sit in on a staff meeting, which he opened by saying, "I highly recommend we get back to our primary task as an organization and creative partnership. We've drifted from what we originally agreed to do, and I don't know where we're headed anymore.

"For example, while I think it's wonderful that we put out a weekly blog post updating customers and the professional community on what we're focusing on, the projects are all over the place, with no consistent thread showing who we are or what we specialize in. I suggest we delete any blogs that veer away from our *essential* concept, tools, and delivery methods."

His speech was met with silence.

This was a controversial suggestion because many people in the room had put intense energy into digital content development to promote the company to new audiences. What Owen didn't share was that the feedback he'd received from clients suggested that the expanded breadth of their interest had confused and muddled their brand. And while Owen didn't seem like a dick in the way he presented this strategy, he came off that way because of what his presentation was meant to accomplish—the silencing of those who had worked hard on the expansive PR campaign.

A week later, Owen called me to discuss what he referred to as "the coup." The aftermath of his unilateral decision apparently resembled a bloody revolution. "We met again and we all behaved badly," he said before launching into a contemptuous and sarcastic diatribe about the "hurt feelings" of those who believed that the company's expansion into new territories should *not* be constrained by an "outdated" mission.

I learned that in his first few meetings with the creative team, Owen made it difficult for anyone else to express their thoughts. Clearly he was angry; what was harder to discern was that he was also hurt. Perhaps his anger was a reaction to his hurt, and the fact he felt uncomfortable revealing his more vulnerable side to his colleagues. When this possibility was posed to Owen, he hit pause to ask himself whether his manner of dealing with the perceived "mutiny" had allowed anyone else to feel like their opinions were heard.

Before, Owen would have acknowledged that *no*, his employees' opinions weren't heard, because they didn't matter. By responding directly to the clients' and partners' concerns, he believed he was protecting the company. But in acting so defensively, he failed to see that he was hostile and uninviting to his staff. Once Owen recognized this, he said, "I felt attacked and betrayed, so I acted accordingly."

Owen had become an executive dick, and several people key to the organization's functionality were now on the verge quitting to launch a competing venture. Dickery in business can easily descend to this point when a leader convinces him or herself that internal opposition should be dismissed.

At the risk of appearing vulnerable, Owen opened up the next staff meeting stating that, "As soon as I proposed the new strategy change, I felt attacked, and that caused me to behave in a way that created, or at least contributed to, an impasse. I see now that I was too adversarial and I want a truce."

The silence that followed *this* comment was more like a pause than a snub.

"I highly recommend we rein in the creative experiments and refocus on our primary task. That said, I regret tyrannizing you to push an agenda that some of you disagree with. I didn't realize I was being a bully. I derailed the creative process. As I said, my feelings were hurt when I thought no one was listening. But I used that disappointment to justify behavior that isn't helping us figure out what to do next."

Owen then proposed a change to the strategy that was less dramatic—more of a recommitment to the approach they'd used before with great success, without deleting anyone's creative work. By accounting for his past behavior, and inviting others to do the same, the office felt again like a safe place to recognize each person's part in what was right and what was not. Others even admitted they had contributed to the company's dysfunction.

Owen and his team are now well versed in the practice of inventory. One would think a team with effective communication tools *shouldn't* revert to the destructive attitudes Owen and his colleagues had resolved, but he acknowledged later that, "The intervention process still allows for a safe space to be dicks—just not to stay that way. And certainly it doesn't force anyone to simply suffer. When we own our issues, we create an environment to communally explore how bad behaviors reflect problems in the organizational dynamic. There may be systematic failures that need to be addressed. It's not necessarily just that someone, in this case me, is a total dick."

Owen and his team were able to intervene in their toxic dynamic and fix it before their bad relations established into a pattern. That's not easy. Sometimes that's not even possible. In fact, when it comes to self-justified behavior, many of us withhold underlying feelings of vulnerability that, if examined, allow us to understand and change our behavior.

EXERCISE: FILLING THE PAUSE BETWEEN THOUGHT AND ACTION

Using the example of Owen and his reactive tyranny, ask yourself: Have there been times when I used hurt feelings to justify behavior that only made things worse?

Think of times when you rationalized conflicts with your emotions. Recall the actions that ensued when you were unable to hit pause and address *your part* in the problem. Has such a process resulted in an attitude that now seems to fuel dickish behavior?

Reflecting on this emotional dynamic, list three behavioral patterns you tend to fall into that have negative consequences. For each one, provide alternative responses that could lead to mutually satisfying outcomes for you and the people you've disagreed with.

1. Pattern/Behavior

_____

_____

Alternative 1.

_____

_____

Alternative 2.

_____

_____

Alternative 3.

_____

_____

2. Pattern/Behavior

_____

_____

Alternative 1.

_____

_____

Alternative 2.

_____

_____

Alternative 3.

_____

_____

3. Pattern/Behavior

_____

_____

Alternative 1.

_____

_____

Alternative 2.

_____

_____

Alternative 3.

_____

_____

Now, let's see what happens when you apply the work you've been doing throughout this process to resolving an issue that has caused you trouble. Look into your history, or at something that is bothering you now, and consider how this book changes your perspective on it. Even just a pet peeve, like for me when people barrel onto the subway before others riders can get out, is worth scrutinizing. Take a look at what causes the issue and how you justify it. Let's address feelings related to the issue and come up with alternative responses.

• THE ISSUE_____

What do you believe actually causes the issue?	How are you hurt, and how do you use that to justify not addressing your role in the problem?	What are your feelings about the harm done to yourself and others?	What can you do to create and sustain alternative responses?

THE ADVANCED COURSE

Now find an issue that's more relative to someone you're close to—a spouse, partner, friend, or family member. Scan your mind for someone you feel comfortable with who might be willing to work with you to address this issue in your relationship. Invite them out with you. To work through that issue together, take an inventory of the relationship and explore how being a dick has interfered with the safety and security in your dynamic.

• THE ISSUE/CONFLICT _____

Together

What kind of reaction did each of you have to the issue? How did you then respond to the other person's reaction?	What was the nature of the harm? How did you each justify not addressing your roles in it?	What are each of your feelings about the incident? Discuss the harm done to each other and the relationship.	How have you both contributed to repairing the harm? What is the result of those efforts?

CHAPTER TWELVE

Fear of Losing Your Dickishness

For years, when one of my clients had a breakthrough in therapy, I would exclaim, "*Bravo!*" That is, until the day a very savvy client said, "Dr. B., it's nice of you to congratulate me for the work I've done. But did you ever consider, what with you being the shrink and all, that in congratulating me, you're actually congratulating yourself? Like, 'Wow, what a great therapist I am! You're actually getting better!'"

Sheeeesh.

Was it really true that when I said "Yay, you!" I actually meant, *Hooray for me*? If so, rather than supportive and caring, I was being a blowhard. Thankfully, I'm pretty sure my client's perception, sharp as it may have been, didn't capture the whole truth. Yet I'm also open to the notion that the truth is more than the eye can see. Letting go of behaviors that offend others, whether we accept their interpretation or not, is tricky, because so many aspects of our behavior are difficult to discern, much less relinquish.

Being a dick can serve to maintain emotional distance, and yet at times angry engagement feels like intimacy. Many couples operate with an emotional distance through which one or both parties are dicks, and therefore neither has to let his or her guard down to see or accept the person hiding beneath the hostility. What this means is that should one or, heaven forbid, both of us drop the dick routine, it would blow up a mutual agreement to use cold behavior to avoid the risk of emotional closeness.

While being a dick protects us from being seen as we actually are, few of us suspect this is what's behind our cold relationships. At the conscious level, we simply believe our partner has been a jerk, and that our own bad behavior is thus justified. However, with many of the couples I see, when one or both of them end their dickery, they often realize their bad behavior has profoundly buried deep insecurities about their own lovability. When the meanness goes away, what's left is the real you—and the challenge of whether you can be accepted as such. This is the trial for many people in long-term relationships. So what happens when we give up our hiding space?

Feet Kicked Out

"Ouch," Marty said. It was a couple's appointment, and his wife Joyce had made an unfavorable comparison between his new beard and those of the millennial hipsters in Brooklyn.

"That hurt?" asked Joyce, feigning innocence.

"It did," Marty said. "My old ability to devalue your opinion isn't working anymore."

"I guess that's progress, right?" Joyce asked.

Marty said, "I used to have mixed feelings, but now I love Joyce, so when she criticizes me, I feel like my feet were kicked out from under me."

"I'm not even sure why I say those things," Joyce said.

"It might start out as a tiny or even accidental kick in the back of my heel," continued Marty. "But when you criticize me, I often trip into a bad mood that lasts all day."

It was much, much worse for Marty and Joyce a couple of years ago, when they hit what they considered their bottom and sought help addressing what was wrong with the relationship. What looked at first like two people simply being dicks to each other turned out to be two people who cared deeply about one another, yet were afraid to acknowledge it.

Joyce said, "It's like I relapse into behavior I don't want to do anymore. Suddenly, I think about all that's happened in the past year. We recommitted ourselves to this relationship. We discovered ways to work out our problems. And now we're trying to have a child."

"Could it be that I still make snarky comments because I'm terrified to be real? When I stopped to check myself for how I contribute to our problems, I saw a way to make things better, and also began to feel how much I cared for Marty. It feels risky, though. Really!"

Bingo! Sometimes holding out hope that things will work out is the scariest prospect of all. We can certainly be dicks to each other when we're scared. But once we create a safe space to account for our part in a problem together, we can use incidents like Joyce and Marty's to expand our security and intimacy with those who threaten us with real closeness. The best way to resist taking someone else's inventory is to take our own. When we keep the focus on ourselves, and our mistakes, it's very difficult to judge, criticize, or in other ways attack each other.

I've seen light bulb after light bulb go off in couples sessions when someone finally gets that this simple-seeming idea is the key to salvaging a relationship that has gone off the rails. Simple as it seems, however, in dick mode it's usually impossible to achieve.

"I'm really sorry for what I said," Joyce told Marty. "I'm so grateful we have ways to analyze how our fears can get the better of us."

Is "Needy" What We Call Folks Whose Needs We Can't Meet?

It's hard to be a dick when you don't use someone else's behavior to justify your bad attitude. And when we put our dickishness down, we begin to feel what was underneath it. Often, what it's protected us from was an awareness of how human we are. There's hardly anything more human than letting go of our defenses and discovering we have vital social needs. If unmet, our needs leave us unhappy, miserable, anxious, and in all likelihood depressed.

We hear all the time, "Don't be needy! You don't want to look desperate." Our culture bombards us with the theory that self-sufficiency is an emotional ideal—a dickish message if I've ever heard one. This notion flies in the face of human nature, which is to rely on other people. We're social creatures who've spent thousands of years surviving in tribes. When we deny this, as we're frequently encouraged to do, we wind up feeling ashamed and humiliated about the emotions that draw us to each other. Healthy relationships require reciprocity and mutuality—what's best described as *interdependence*. Again, our dickery pushes that oh-so-human need to belong and feel accepted out of our awareness. Rather than heed the call for care and affection, then, we deny our humanity.

So, when we call our partners "needy," are we actually announcing that we're unable to meet their needs? In other words, are we being dicks?

Of course, not all dependency is good dependency. There are healthy and unhealthy—mature versus infantile—forms of "neediness." The Scottish psychoanalyst W. Ronald D. Fairbairn explored and understood personal development in terms of social dependency. Whereas Freud believed humans were primarily pleasure-seeking creatures, Fairbairn saw us as *object* seeking, or what we might think of us now as relationship seeking. That means we seek to relate to others based on interactions modeled to us at an early age. Fairbairn theorized that all meaningful human activity, from the most primitive act to the highest emotional expression, is connected to relationships, be those with actual people in the external world, or memories and fantasies of people in our interior world. He believed self-expression in a relationship was the ultimate human goal.

Fairbairn, along with the analysts of his time who identified as *interpersonal psychoanalysts*, profoundly influenced the most contemporary model of psychoanalysis—relational psychoanalysis. Our contemporary notion of healthy adult development now almost invariably includes interdependence with others. Intense closeness with loved ones in particular is seen as ideal. In such relationships, it's an acknowledged virtue to be dependable and able *to depend on* a partner. Fairbairn, in labeling the highest level of human development "mature dependence," emphasized the importance of trusting and loving relationships.

Yet "dependency" still seems like a dirty word, making the distancing aspect of dickish behavior harder to remedy. Embracing healthy dependence means that the person who threatens to *matter* gets to see your vulnerable side. The fear of losing your dickish behavior is conveyed as a fear of appearing *weak*. That's what the term "needy" has come to mean: *weak*. But expressing dependence on another person is about the basic human need to belong, feel cared for, and be accepted. When we're in touch with those feelings, we don't want to attack others, lest we disrupt our sense of care and validation.

Adios, MF

Being a dick can happen unexpectedly during life-changing transitions, like when a good friend is moving away. Under duress, emotional distances can develop. This often feels like an eruption, a spontaneous reaction to challenging feelings.

These more subtle forms of psychological defense are often situational. They develop, for instance, as an unstated coldness pact between two people on a first date who feel overwhelmed by desperation and desire. The sense of disinvestment protects them both from the shame of potential rejection. It can also happen in a young company when key stakeholders curb progress to manage the anxiety that, after all this time, success might actually be possible.

Ron and Phillip had been best friends for eighteen years, and when Ron announced he was moving away, Phillip faced severe heartbreak.

"I have to say, I didn't see it coming," Phillip shared. "Ron just disappeared. He had attended both of my weddings, and he consoled me for hours when the first one tanked. I sat crying on his couch for a whole weekend while he listened patiently and nursed me back to life. He was even there in the waiting room during the birth of both of my kids."

"He just up and moved?" I asked. "No warning?"

"No, I knew he was planning to leave," Phillip admitted. "But I didn't think he would also dismiss our friendship on his way out. Now that I think about it, he'd been behaving worse and worse. My kids refer to him as 'Uncle Ron,' so he disappointed them with the increased absence as well, and I have to wonder if we aren't better off without him."

"I see. But still you're shocked?"

"Of course," Phillip said. "Yet something had been amiss ever since I called his move an 'escape.' Even though I took the comment back immediately, I'd never seen him so mad."

"And now *you're* devaluing the friendship," I said.

"Is that what I'm doing?" Phillip asked. "I guess I'm hurt."

The devaluing of a person, situation, or relationship doesn't strictly occur in the form of unkind behavior. But that's how the dickishness we use to protect ourselves manifests.

"It's just painful to feel Ron disappearing from my life," Phillip said.

"So you're trying to scrub him from your heart, pulling the same maneuver he pulled."

"After all we've been through, it's mind-boggling," said Phillip.

"Or not," I countered. "Because you're both trying to protect your feelings."

Let's rethink Phillip's "escape" comment to Ron. It seems like his remark *really* said: I'm going to miss you so much that, rather than put it in words, I'll express it in dickish behavior that I hope stops you from leaving and calms my sense of abandonment.

What to do instead is not easy—say what you really feel.

"Really," said Phillip, "all I want to say to Ron now is, *Adios, MF.*"

"MF?"

"*My Friend.*"

I had to chuckle at that.

Agreements (One Last Time)

Throughout this book we've been looking at the *agreements* we have between ourselves and the world—if/then statements that we've used to justify our dickish behavior. We now see that many of these agreements are no more than contingency plans to legitimize our bad actions. But in this chapter, we found a rationale for dickery that's more thoughtful and compassionate. Our dickish behavior often comes from a place of love, but acts out our need to protect ourselves from being hurt and scared.

Now that we've pinpointed our agreements and revised them to envision a future self who is comfortable in our own skin and in healthy relationships with the world, let's take another look at this process. We now have the opportunity to change our agreements.

Much is made about being ready for change. But after working for many years as a therapist in Southern California and in New York City, I can say that *willingness* is far more important than readiness. Readiness can lead to endless postponement by our psychological defenses. But willingness is stronger than that. So with all the willingness you can muster, take another pass at your *agreements* with the world, and see if you can develop an outlook driven by optimism.

In the long run, to not be a dick is to take it easy on the world and those around you. By now I hope you also understand, though, that the one you're really taking it easy on, coming to terms with, and learning to accept is you.

For the final example, we'll look at the two most common agreements I've seen throughout my research into the subject of dicks, and how *not to be one*. These agreements are bedrock for most of us because they tap into the most vulnerable thing about being human. And while these agreements make sense, it will be among the greatest gifts that we can give to ourselves if we can catch ourselves making them, hit pause, and find better ways to respond.

EXERCISE: AGREEMENTS

Agreement	How this plays out in my behavior toward others	The impact on how I relate to others and am perceived
Example A: When people scare me, I attack.	When I'm scared I convince myself that the person I'm closest to is to blame and I attack them.	I've attained a reputation as an "angry person" and, though it's me who is scared, I'm told that I'm the scary one.
Example B: When people hurt me, I run.	When I'm hurt and unable to understand why, I immediately shut down.	I'm considered standoffish and impossible to reach. But instead of seeing I'm hurt, people think I'm apathetic or arrogant.

Using the above examples as a reference (and your responses in Chapters One and Seven), write down two or three of your own agreements—perhaps revised and revised again—that you've made with the world. Hurt and fear are generally the cornerstones to the insecurities that justify dickery, so pay special attention to whether you have any agreements that relate to being hurt or scared. Then answer the following questions:

- How rigid are these agreements—and the attitudes and actions that go with them?

- Is it possible that these agreements have put you in a position to be more hurt or more scared?

- How malleable might these agreements be?

- Might the transformation we are seeking come from changing the agreements that exist between us and the world? What might that look like?

CHAPTER THIRTEEN

Yippee I'm Not a Dick!

Is it cause for celebration when a dick finally puts down their weapons and becomes reasonable? Of course! But many people who halt destructive behaviors learn that the world is unlikely to throw you a parade for playing nice. This is largely because what most dicks believe is exceptionally nice, friendly behavior is what a majority of society considers normal, expected behavior.

So by all means, celebrate your heart out. Dance, sing, and pat yourself on the back. But don't expect to receive kudos. Obviously, it's a great thing you're no longer a dick, it's just that:

- You may have chased away the people best suited to assess and congratulate the transformation.

- You still have amends to make, and it's unlikely the people you've hurt will celebrate your change.

- These changes are meant to stop you from hurting yourself as much as anyone else.

- Opening up to a new dynamic with the world is its own reward.

One of the great benefits of being a dick in recovery is the ability to recognize what's behind the dickish behavior in your midst. With your newfound, better behavior, you might act as proof to others that *there is another way*. You might also suss out a willingness in others to change.

We know there are a lot of jerks out there. And now we *also* know that there's no better way to attract them than to act like one ourselves. It may be tempting to imagine some kind of loophole that will allow us to slip back into minor incidents of dickery and then return to our newfound harmony with the world. But that's not possible. The dicks are still out there—right where they were when we began this journey—and, like relapse into any other compulsive behavior, one act of dickery is not enough and a thousand is too many. Slipping back into dickery encourages others to once again see and react to us in ways that are destructive and completely out of our control. Dickery begets dickery. All the hard work in the world will not change that. We can, however, use this information, and the hard work we've done so far, to avoid relapse as we duck and cover against the rampant dickery in the world.

Judge and Jury, No More

Holding expectations for how others should respond to our admission of bad behavior and commitment to change sets us up for disappointment and righteous indignation—a slippery slope back toward the justifications we used to be a dick.

There's a twelve-step saying that "whenever we are disturbed, no matter what the cause, there is something wrong with us." That may sound like bad news. But when we realize what is wrong with us, we can do something about it. Our sense of disturbance can act as a warning light, telling us, ideally with gentleness, we have a need that is unmet, an insecurity for which we need comfort, a hurt we need to heal. And this awareness that dickery places us in a position to be hurt empowers us:

1. To understand how our acting-out behavior and denial impacts our world, and account for that one relationship at a time

2. To hit pause and decline invitations to dickery, even when we feel justified to counterattack

3. To make the world a better place for others and ourselves

I can't tell you how many times couples have sat on my couch and tried to make me their judge and jury. In those cases, the couples don't want to fix their relationship so much as they want an objective authority figure to confirm one of them is right, pound the gavel, and issue a guilty verdict declaring the other person wrong, and then punish their partner for making them miserable.

What a sad state of affairs it would be if the point of therapy was to confirm that your aggression is justified, and your only hope to get better lies in other people behaving themselves. That to me would be the height of helplessness.

I've found that in the first session of couple's therapy, each person often starts with a list of offenses committed by the other person. It's so common, in fact, that after many years of doing this, I can accurately predict what each person wants to say before we even start. I'll tell them, "What you want to share now is a history of grave injustices committed by your partner, with whom you feel misunderstood and unheard—and that goes for both of you. I'm sure you believe you'd be best served if we held a sort of trial here. But I'm afraid that's not really what therapy is about. If history has taught me anything, it's that the best way I can serve you is to let you know you *have a right to be wrong* in your marriage. If we work together, we can establish a safe place for you to assess, claim, and own what you've contributed to the brokenness you feel in your relationship."

Usually, I get blank stares at that point. Then the partners tussle verbally to see who gets to launch their diatribe against the other first.

So it went with Joel and Allison, who upon entering therapy had reached a point at which they could not have a conversation with each other without it devolving into an argument. Each was thoroughly convinced that the other was to blame for their problems. Joel believed none of his good deeds went unpunished; Allison felt like Joel disregarded everything she said or did as valueless. They each felt hurt, angry, and insulted, feelings that justified endless dickish behavior, which triggered poor treatment back and forth.

After we worked together for a few months, they finally got my point. Worn down by the sheer intensity of what had become a standoff, they looked at how they each fed into their pain. This realization began when Joel discussed what he believed were kind, generous, and caretaking actions on his part. He had been diminishing Allison by leaving no room for her to make valuable contributions to the relationship, he realized. Allison then admitted that one reason she fell in love with Joel was that he came across as "rescuer," willing—and seemingly able—to save her from her painful history and whatever else might arise. Yet as time went on, she found this behavior embarrassing and insulting, as she was constantly treated like a helpless victim.

"Like Dr. B said, it isn't working for us when all we do is try to convince him that one of us is right and the other person is wrong," Joel said.

"Well, we were past the point of convincing each other."

"Only when being awful seemed like something I did *with* Allison, rather than *to* her, did it seem possible for me to stop and understand what was happening." Joel added.

"When Joel stopped trying to save me," Allison said, "I could see that allowing him to look like an a-hole was not very nice of me. I let him fall flat on his face over and over again. I had figured out that if I kept my mouth shut, Joel would keep talking and make himself look worse and worse. But that wasn't kind of me."

For quite some time, because of the dynamic Allison confessed to, it was difficult for them to share responsibility for what was wrong. Once they did, after an honest appraisal of their relationship, they saw the contributions they each made to what was *right* about their relationship as well.

It's an old pop-psych-meets-Freudian truism that we tend to gravitate toward romantic partners who remind us of—or are just like—our opposite-sex parent. But while many of us *do* find qualities in our long-term partner that are familiar, I find often that we rather marry into our unresolved family conflicts. It provides a chance to repair wounds we bring with us.

When Joel and Allison created a shared space of intimacy and safety, they broke out of their compulsions to be dicks, and experienced their love as a source of healing that they didn't even recognize was available.

Proclamations of Non-Dickery

You're leaping further along the road of recovery now. Keep in mind the work you've done throughout this process as you explore the following proclamations, which were developed specifically to keep you on track.

Read them aloud and refer back to them when necessary. They will remind you of what's important, in case you lose your bearings.

Changing habitual patterns is not easy, so take these proclamations to heart. They embody health and growth, and are about community. There are others out there who are recovering from dickery along with you. This is about letting go of behaviors that isolate you, and about building interpersonal connections. The proclamations are written to be inclusive instead of exclusive. With the insights you've attained so far, they can serve as reminders to continue making amends and righting the wrongs that occur in relationships. These efforts are an archway that leads out of loneliness and depression.

PROCLAMATION #1: WE'RE CHANGING THIS VERY MINUTE!

We're interested in real changes to the circumstances, environments, and relationships in our personal and community life. By improving our ability to interact with the world and by making difficult choices, such as to spend less time with destructive friends, find better ways to spend our time, or look for a new job or career, we expand our sense of self.

In discovering that we've been caught in a cycle of being a dick or the target of dickery, we can challenge this structure, expand our awareness of our isolation, and recognize how dickish behavior stops us from achieving things we actually want, like intimate relationships.

We have awareness, now, of how we've chosen partners who would join in this routine. We get how we created a state of dickery, which was like an airtight seal, enclosing us in a defensive pattern.

We've defined dickery as a relationship with the world, as represented by its people, that blocks us from intimacy and ensures that in relationships we do *not* experience our true thoughts and feelings regarding our underlying fear of rejection and abandonment.

Like a parasite that makes its host hungry for trouble, our dickery creates the context in which we sustain our isolating patterns of defensive behavior and perception. But at least we now know there are alternatives.

We see how self-awareness of pain, fear, loneliness, and the ways we previously managed these experiences, open windows of opportunity to change, both within ourselves and in concert with the people we surround ourselves with. This transformation is the cornerstone of growth and healing through repair. It leads to a reciprocal give-and-take, to mutuality.

Rather than reject opportunities because they're scary or daunting and react with destructiveness, we behave with compassion for ourselves and others. We've become empowered to take a stand against our demons and reclaim the right to life that we had stolen from ourselves.

PROCLAMATION #2: WE ARE HONEST WITH OURSELVES ABOUT THE CAUSES AND CONDITIONS OF OUR BEHAVIOR

The best way to deal with a problem is to understand what causes it and eliminate the cause. This is true for the protective mechanisms we developed during childhood, which cause the same problems we use them to block out. When we were young, and to some degree still, we felt overloaded with an anxiety that made it difficult to function. So we created defensive routines that preempted being rejected, abandoned, or mistreated. We were the ones to wield power against the world. We became dicks. This worked to dissociate the anxiety. But it stopped working when we developed broader mental and emotional skills and became adults dealing with other adults. We haven't used our new emotional range until now, because part of our defense was to forget we had built it up. We assumed dickishness was just a part our character ("who I am").

It's like we locked something precious in a safe and forgot the combination—our vulnerability was safe, even from us! Addressing the ways we ward off our awareness of anxiety will help to prevent relapse; when we detect the subtle signals that warn us of potential triggers, we know we're in danger of behaving dickishly and need to hit pause. Considering the significance of this phenomenon, we must focus on our reactions to stressful situations and make changes.

PROCLAMATION #3: WE HAVE NEW ROLES

Recovering from being a dick necessitates looking within. Our defensive operations—the sum total of our psychological defenses, and how they manifest in our lives—by now are increasingly impossible to ignore. When examined through inventory, we can see the many roles we take on and understand how our defenses contain anxiety and subvert important aspects of ourselves. It sounds convoluted, but it's the truth!

Once freed from the prison of being a dick, we begin to explore our old roles and discover thoughts, feelings, and ways of behaving that we never had a chance to experience before. We can create spaces for new growth. In a way, this process is like erosion; cycles of freezing and heating create cracks in hard rocks, where seedlings take root and further widen the crevices until the boulders break apart.

We also become more socially nimble. As more trust grows, we can relate to other people in less anxious and confining ways. Things feel less rigid when there are fewer rules to break. Our anxiety lessens. We begin to experience ourselves as members of real relationships, ones that we can let matter, in communion with each other, our families, our communities, and the world around us. We aren't stuck in our dickery. There is room to be alive.

PROCLAMATION #4: WE CONTRIBUTE TO THE SOLUTION

As we come to terms with the dick in ourselves and our patterns of relating, we can account for not only how we contribute to problems, but also how we can contribute to solutions. We can work through our negative feelings, dysfunctional behaviors, and chronic problems by participating in "asset mapping" to assess our current state of health and identify resources for recovery. We can discover areas of self-esteem and empowerment. By looking at our history of defending these resources, we can strengthen and focus them in positive ways. Asset mapping is a key component of constructive self-analysis.

Asset mapping identifies our growing resourcefulness and resiliency. It's a simple commitment to look to the positive and healthy elements of ourselves, our relationships, and the world that exists around us for the strength to live our lives fully, in acceptance of ourselves and our conditions.

We can also recognize that feeling pain is a way to move toward a solution. It's like an SOS signal. Pain says we're suffering from isolation. Necessity is the mother of invention, and so the initial assets we develop are built upon the rock bottom we've hit. Eventually an emotional experience breaks through our defenses, propelling us toward recovery, health, and true community.

It's beneficial to understand our relationship patterns from within the system that developed them and the conditioned thinking habits that sustain them. When we really understand our dickery, we can see precisely how our defenses operate in the moment, and use this knowledge to stop repeating our reactions to our fear of rejection and abandonment. Rather than living through our defensive structure, we experience a transformative shift in how our emotions work.

At these moments, we can have a dialogue with ourselves we didn't have before about what we're up to, and we can exercise more control over what we decide to do. In short, we can make new choices. Furthermore, at those crucial moments, if we have a good idea of what a better choice might look like, we are more likely to pick that path, moving toward being in authentic and genuine relationship with others as well as ourselves.

PROCLAMATION #5: WE COME FROM OUR ASSETS

We have done exercises throughout this book to help identify our resources, recognize how we need to look at things differently, and consider ways to make alternative choices to shift the dynamic within ourselves and with other people. By pinpointing our assets, we can move through anxiety-inducing experiences, and defuse our knee-jerk reactions.

We choose to address our strengths. Our resources, abilities, and resilience are on par with or above our problems. We need to look at what's *right* with those around us and with ourselves even more than what's wrong. The best way to start might be to revise our perception of the "dys" all around us—a lens of dysfunction. We grow freer as we recognize what is functional.

Acknowledging our assets and developing new and more constructive skills will help when we doubt whether we have what it takes to achieve better relationships. And we do! By changing the way we respond to the world, we also challenge old perceptions of threat in relationships and our experience of anxiety. Sometimes this means being different with the same people, and sometimes it means being with different people entirely. Truth be told, we're built to tolerate a fairly high dose of anxiety. We're highly resilient even if the way our brains deal with reality can sometimes lead to vicious cycles. Building walls to protect ourselves from awareness of anxiety has unfortunately also protected us from knowing how durable we are.

We traded flexible resilience for brittle resilience, becoming hard so we could resist strong forces. We felt unready to develop an ability to bend to avoid breaking. But we have what it takes to survive our tumultuous histories. We can lower defenses, soften our reactions to anxiety, and open up to serendipity and delight.

PROCLAMATION #6: WE NEED EACH OTHER TO BE EMPOWERED

The insights and exercises in this book were meant to promote an empowerment built to last. This kind of empowerment takes work, but with time that work becomes habit. We know empowerment is an inside job, but we also know the outside world reflects what's going on inside us. Empowerment must come from within, but it cannot exist in isolation. Our world is so thoroughly social, the idea of personal empowerment that doesn't incorporate relationships is delusional.

The myth of total self-sufficiency is destructive. To function independently, we must learn to rely on others. We only obtained a rudimentary, fragile sense of empowerment by protecting our self-esteem. And since this brittle empowerment is shored up by the same defenses that kept us isolated from others in dickish behavior, it's not useful at all. Empowerment that is mere egotism leads to resentment, indignation, and cycles of dickery—not empowerment at all, but a shoring-up of our old, isolating habit of self-sufficiency. Seeing this facet of ourselves requires a shift in thinking and the courage to investigate parts of ourselves that are unprocessed in our relationships with the people who matter.

Now, think about the following questions:

1. What was it like to read the proclamations aloud?

2. What new proclamations might you want to make? Go ahead, make them!

3. Why not experiment with optimistic thoughts and behaviors and see how they affect your life? Make a list of statements that make you feel good, and use these proclamations to practice intentionally having a more optimistic outlook.

CONCLUSION

Both the Cause and the Cure

I hope it has turned out to be a good thing that the person you bought this book for returned it and said, "You might want to read this too."

One more thing. You're going to wipe out. You're going to get this wrong, blow it, tank, fail. Down in flames you'll go. And that's okay. It happens and there's no way around it.

Don't panic. When you first experience tumbling back into your dick routine, you'll likely feel like you're "wearing dog shoes"—a term used by SoCal surfer dudes for a person who just had a severe wipeout. Though slung about like an insult, being told you're wearing dog shoes should make you proud. There's something to be said about having the biggest, gnarliest wipeout—oh, and being *seen* doing so—because that means that despite not being the best surfer ever, you're putting yourself out there. Cowabunga! You're going for it!

It might seem odd that wiping out, and then trying again with the help of others, would be a goal for recovery. But breaking out of isolation can feel like breaking some kind of law, the law of dickery, which decrees that thou shalt *not* genuinely communicate with others, lest the anxiety that comes with caring about people befall you. So we wipe out, turn to each other for help in the recovery, and then do it all over again.

Initially, there's an ironic dilemma to not being a dick:

1. You're no longer good at being a dick.

2. But you're not good at *not* being a dick, either.

There's a lot of fine print in romantic relationship about how intimate we've agreed to be. While being a dick causes emotional distance, at times the heated, angry engagement actually feels intimate. In reality, this is but a substitute for intimacy. Wearing dog shoes in romance means exposing those feelings about ourselves that have historically come out through bad behavior—distancing, off-putting, downright dickish actions—and finally using what had been a wipeout as an opportunity to heal old wounds together.

Indeed, when wearing dog shoes as a recovering dick, the goal is to work through the dynamics that made dickery somewhat bearable. This road is one on which we can expect to wipe out often. Success requires immense amounts of perseverance, as we get back on the board, struggle to paddle through the breakers to a new set, and attempt to stand, knowing we may fall yet again.

One of my favorite quotes on this sort of tenacity comes from Samuel Beckett, in his novella *Worstward Ho*:

"Ever tried. Ever failed. No matter. Try again. Fail again. Fail better."

Home to Roost

What happens when we do hit bottom? When we wake up, say, in a long-term relationship and realize the impact our bad behavior has had on ourselves and others?

"I can't help the fact that for the past decade your financial contributions to this family have sucked!" said Jerome.

"What?" Gina yelled. "You apologize right now! You claim you're making amends, but I've told you many times how hurtful it is when you hold your income over me. You constantly demean my contributions."

"Okay, so I apologize, I take responsibility for my behavior, and I tell you I'm going to change, then you attack?" Jerome countered.

"No—you admit to *some* behavior," Gina said. "I still have intense feelings about how you've treated me. You think you can just instantly take everything back?"

"No," admits Jerome, "I realize it's not that easy. And I wasn't trying to withhold a full apology. I'm just not good at this."

Look, the people in your world are likely to have feelings about your past behavior, and if they feel safe doing so, they may very well express them. That sounds scary, I know, but there's a silver lining.

"I've hung in this for a long time believing there's a good soul hiding beneath that awful attitude," Gina said. "I've wanted to believe there's more to my part, too, than stubborn masochism."

"It has been scary to let my guard down," admitted Jerome. "And expecting you to respond graciously to my amends, *or else*, maybe caused me to revert to my old, unkind ways."

Hearing others share their experiences of what it's been like to be around a dick is rough.

"I'm at my worst when I'm worried about money," Jerome said. "I'm so afraid of being unable to provide for us that I take it out on you."

"You do!"

"I don't know how to deal with this," Jerome said. "But I'm sure that dealing with it by myself is killing me."

As we've explored throughout this book, when we're dicks we invite *engagement* from others, but we're overly protective against an attack, which eventually comes in the form of what is in fact a *counterattack*. Living that way can be the loneliest thing imaginable. And this is true even when we're married. Sometimes, depending on how resistant we are to allowing ourselves to be cared for, we can feel isolated in psychotherapy as well.

"It isn't just killing you," Gina said. "It's killing *us*."

What this tension does, however, is create an opening to express the pain, fear, sadness, and disappointment we've been living with for all that time.

"Let me try this again," Jerome said.

Repair

Developing a healthy relationship, with a strong, secure attachment, is not a linear process. In fact, some of the steps along the way to a functional relationship are painful fits and starts. We tend to think failures to connect, trust, or be empathetic signal doom and gloom ahead.

Yet on the contrary, these are opportunities to right wrongs together and put the train back on the rails.

Developmental theorist Edward Tronick believed "rupture and repair" was the cornerstone of health.[40] It's not the smooth flow of harmonious interaction that leads to healthy attachment, Tronick stated. It's disruptions between the two parties that eventually lead to mutually agreeable resolutions or repairs.

As psychologist David Belford explains it in his paper "Breaks in the Flow:"

> Attachment theory tells us that when parents respond to their infants cries in a more or less consistent, predictable and nurturing way, the infant will begin to build a sense a [sic] trust and safety in their world ("I know I will be taken care of"). The repetition of these types of experiences of being responded to builds and reinforces "healthy" neural pathways in the infant's brain. In much the same way, through the repeated process of disruption and repair, the infant adds to his knowledge or blueprint of the nature of relationships, increases his tolerance for stress, and begins to realize a sense of agency in the world. The disorganization or dysregulation that follows a disruption and the subsequent repair of that disruption is part of the infant's development and crucial to building secure attachments. It is the chief mechanism by which the infant begins to make meaning of relationships.

My client Tyler dealt with the impact of an insecure attachment style for decades. "I couldn't stay in a relationship for longer than nine months," he said. "For the longest time, it felt like something was wrong with me, some basic capacity was missing. At that point, my interest—sexual and otherwise—completely fell off. Of course, it didn't feel like something was wrong in the moment. It seemed like the flaws were hers. And that's when I'd act like a stereotypical dick." He paused. "Then I met Isabella. Funny thing about her—she could be just as big a dick as me."

Eureka!

As a partner, Isabella continues to interest Tyler. But as much as I believe in the importance of a good fit, their compatibility has less to do with mutual dickishness than it does a relational dynamic that frequently requires both participants to put down their weapons and diligently repair the damage they've caused one another. They argue, fight, and trigger bouts of insecurity and conflict in one another. And these patterns of relating finally did allow them to *see* and experience their ruptures as opportunities to repair together.

Rupture, ironically enough, is the royal road to the kind of repair that allowed Isabella and Tyler to heal from the dickish damage they were causing each other. When they got a good foothold on doing inventory and committing themselves to the process of rupture and repair, they could look into their own histories and discover the real damage of their dickery was to themselves.

"She kicked my ass—and my heart," Tyler exclaimed.

Love as Transformation

If you think about it, the very first form of love we experience is attention. Without having it from birth and in something approximating the right dose, we will die.

Is being a dick therefore about seeking love? Is it like Goldilocks, a matter of finding one that's "just right," or when starved, going to dramatic and often backfiring lengths to obtain such attention?

Maybe, but most of all *not being a dick* allows us to love and be loved—what my colleagues and I have refer to as "relationship sanity" in our book by the same name. Relationship sanity is contingent on functional dependence on one another. The truth is, we can adjust to difficult circumstances, so when we're hating deeply, it's less about whatever seems wrong in others and more about what we cannot stand in ourselves. It's human nature to judge each other. But if we recognize and accept that this is as much a judgment of our own shortcomings, failures, and dickery, we'll be far more willing to have compassion and empathy for others and ourselves.

EXERCISE: IMPLETIVE—ONE LAST TIME

Once I understood what being a dick was all about, the time between me recognizing someone as a dick and reacting to them dwindled down to nearly nothing. What do I care, at this point, if you're a dick? I have zero control over that. Me on the other hand, with *Don't Be a Dick* at the ready, I can prevent myself from having a bad day, each and every day.

So one last time, without overthinking it, write down the words you've used to fill in the blank for *#@!%*:

1. _____

2. _____

3. _____

Stone Cold Dick

I haven't been speaking about physical violence, infidelity, or criminal behavior because the ways of the dick are such that everyone in the world knows they're a dick. Everyone, that is, except the dick. And the above-listed extremes don't qualify as subtle or easily hidden from the self.

It's possible that being a dick has worked fine for you, that it gives you *street cred* or money from the passive income you gain through doing minimal work at the expense of your underlings. You don't kill people, cool. But you don't empathize with others, either. So along with wielding what feels like superior power, you maintain emotional distance that protects you from those gut-punches in life that occur when someone you care about goes through a hard time, especially when all that can be done is to listen and love that person.

You won't have to worry about vulnerability; it comes from trusting others will not hurt you due to past harm or envy. And even though being a dick invites counterattacks, our armor is strong. Security flaws are unlikely because no one can exploit what they know about us. No one knows a dick.

So many common, easily overlooked (or, self-justified) ways to be a dick, right? Glaring at people who annoy us, line-cutting, sulking, silent scorn, making unreasonable demands, and offering uninvited "constructive criticism." They all seem to do the same thing: Put us dead center in other people's line of fire. Being a dick makes you a moving target, and as a moving target you won't have to worry about sinking roots into a relationship. And the sum of this mighty effort—as we've seen, it's actually tough to be a dick, especially a stone cold one—is that intimacy, accepting ourselves and others as we are, is out of the question. Being a dick is a powerful defense against that most stereotypical human fear: intimacy.

Almost any circumstance in our lives can threaten us with intimacy. In the process of living our lives, there is always the chance that we might get to know each other. See and be seen.

Living the gamble of vulnerability—rolling the dice on acceptance or rejection in each new encounter—is harrowing business. Perhaps that scary question from kindergarten—*Do you like me?*—is still with us. In the crosshairs of other people's responses to our need to be cared for and accepted, our most primitive terrors come forward. Uncertain outcomes that seem as random as a coin flip—heads you like me, tails you don't— tempt us to be dicks. Hostility is an effective way to manage anxiety, as it dissociates awareness of the fear that vulnerability exposes us to. If you're a stone cold dick, you might need to take creative measures to avoid this pitfall. Get a plant or pet fish, or something else to help commit yourself to keeping something fragile and vulnerable alive.

Though we all act like dicks from time to time, and while we have a tremendous capacity to inflict heartache and pain, we are also natural healers of the wounds we cause and bear in our relationships.

Satyagraha

Let me tip my hand, fully, and admit that writing this book has been my form of *Satyagraha*, a nonviolent resistance to my own dickery. While I've preferred to share anecdotes of other people managing their dickery, I can't ignore my own reactions to a certain SNAFU that ground me down for years. Through analysis, I've discovered that I was recently driven by a terrible sense of being un-okay with the people I worked with. This anxious, counter-productive energy manifested in me trying to impose my will to get a collaborative project off the ground.

We'd experienced modest success in a previous project, and the next thing I knew I couldn't *let* things happen as we had before. Instead, I felt driven to *make* success occur. We were a small rag-tag group of healthcare professionals trying to force our goose to lay golden eggs. But I forgot to that in simply coming together with people I admired for a project we all cared about, we were already okay.

I forced that project, the team, and myself to contort into shapes that made us all feel insecure, angry, unappreciated, and even vengeful. Eventually, we were all trying to make a fairly successful and enjoyable project become something else. At that point I started to despise the thing. I wanted to kill the project and my colleagues. Everyone was acting like a dick, I thought. And they thought the same of me.

When I found myself blowing my top at an East Village restaurant at a partner who, I believed in the moment, needed to "Shut the f—k up," I was able to acknowledge that I'd hit bottom. In that moment, I became what an old mentor of mine called "sweetly reasonable"—willing to put the shovel down and stop digging.

It didn't help that some family friends were sitting at a nearby table shielding their eyes to spare me the embarrassment of being seen acting like a dick. Finally, I paused and committed myself to *Satyagraha*, which is Sanskrit and Hindi for "holding onto truth." A philosophy of nonviolent resistance to evil (or for our purposes, dickery), Satyagraha can be applied to civil disobedience, to seeking alternative political and economic systems, and to correct daily living. Satyagraha conquers through conversion, offering neither victory nor defeat but rather a new harmony. It goes beyond simply not harming those who we believe have harmed us.

Satyagraha was utilized in two of the most significant movements against oppression of the 20th Century: The struggle against British colonization in India led by Mahatma Gandhi, and the Civil Rights Movement in the United States led by Martin Luther King, Jr. Both Gandhi and King took inspiration from this nonviolent philosophy to accomplish what had previously seemed impossible. Even violence was met with nonviolence. And yet each man's society resisted the dramatic cultural and political transformation away from violent oppression. The success of Satyagraha relies ultimately on the willingness of its opponent to relinquish power in favor of a higher ethical standard. Yet in systems of oppression, nonviolence is an undesirable, alien response. The assassinations of Gandhi and MLK sadly prove how challenging and revolutionary such a stance may be.

Neither leader wavered on his commitment to peace, and each remained conscientious of the well-being of his violent oppressor. Gandhi once told followers to desist from protesting at 2 p.m. each day because it exposed the fair-skinned British soldiers to harsh sunlight, an act of violence in his eyes. Depriving ourselves and others from positivity via dickish behavior is likewise a violent act.

As I see it, Satyagraha is a resistance to acting like a dick, *especially* when that behavior seems justified. Reframing what could be seen as passive aggressiveness, Satyagraha has the potential to transform stonewalling into something productive and constructive—a *pause*. The idea of Satyagraha is not just to "live and let live," but to "live and *help* live." Therefore, it wasn't sufficient for my colleagues and I to simply walk away from our destructive business relationship. To commit to Satyagraha meant pausing what felt like a downward spiral, and during that pause we each kept the focus on ourselves. We found a willingness, then, to treat each other and the project with proper care and respect. But like in recovery from any other compulsive or addictive substance or behavior, what we got wasn't some healed-for-all-time solution, but rather more of a reprieve we had to renew on a daily basis.

"One day at a time," I sometimes said to myself. "I won't hit the self-destruct button on this project *today*." Satyagraha allowed us to take inventory and arrive at respectful collaborative solutions to the issues that arose between us *one day at a time*.

This book has been my response—not reaction—to a dickery that temporarily derailed and nearly destroyed a project I loved. I'm showing up. I understand this is the first and most essential step to being okay—

living comfortably in my own skin and accepting the world and myself exactly as we are.

How Will You Be Remembered?

"Loving, kind, and generous," says Mike. "That's how I want to be remembered by my kids and grandkids. My grandmother was that way to me, and thinking of her has me wondering what words or feelings will come to mind when others remember me."

There is a shorthand way we're held in other's hearts.

Think about your parents, grandparents, childhood friends, teachers, and a person who hurt you, like say your first love. How do you describe them in conversation? How do you describe them to yourself? Who is this person to you? If each of us gets just a few descriptive words in the hearts and minds of those we care about, we should act consistently in accordance with what we wish those words to be.

Like my client Mike, it's good to consider what our legacies will be now. "I talk to my wife, Hannah, about it when I realize I've been critical of my kids," he said.

That might sound like a suggestion to constrain your behavior to that of a good, upstanding, wholesome person. Just, you know, to not be a dick. But it's not that simple or easy. How we're held in others' hearts and minds is not just about what we *give*—that is, the good or bad we express—but how we accept what others offer us, bond, and allow each other to matter. Letting others contribute to our experience has a different value than simply spraying our supposed generosity all over everyone while we keep the significance and value of what others provide to a minimum.

Mike knew this. As a teenager, he argued frequently with his parents, and at one point he ran away from home and moved in with the group of friends that he and his parents had been fighting about. Predictably, with those "rough kids," he partook in all kinds of destructive behavior.

"I didn't know how to stop," he once recalled to me. "Nor could I ask for help. Within a month, I felt like I was dying. I'm not sure how she found me, but one day my grandmother knocked on the door. Some wasted kid opened it. She asked for me, and I stumbled downstairs, and she said, 'Mike, you know I could really use some company.'"

Mike shared this through tears.

"That was all she said. Something about this coming right when I felt completely betrayed and alone got to me. She wasn't trying to play the do-gooder there to rescue me—my parents actually forbid her from interfering—she made it clear I would be helping her feel less lonely. We would get through what was happening in our dysfunctional family together. I was on a dark path, but this changed that trajectory for me."

Perhaps not being a dick comes more naturally to people like Mike's grandmother than it does to others. But when we consider the impact our behavior has on others, we might think once again about how an inventory doesn't have to be scribbled in red ink. We might pause to remember that not being a dick is not just about preventing ourselves from getting our asses kicked, it's also about inviting care, concern, and love from potential allies.

"There were many times in the early years of my marriage and when I first became a parent that I harped on the message to, 'Look at everything I do for you.'" Mike said. "I went on and on about the time and money and career moves I'd sacrificed to be a more involved father and husband. I focused narrowly on how much I gave rather than on what I received. I was insufferable, a complete dick. I had to pause—as you suggested—and remember how my grandmother became the warm, loving presence that lives on in my head. The last thing she would ever do was try to convince me of all the good she'd done for me—how loving and generous she was. Instead, she showed me."

Mike's grandmother was about as far from being a dick as is humanly possible. But she still was somehow able to get the message across that not being a dick can leave a legacy that inspires others to be kind to each other. Actions like hers have a domino effect through time, influencing how people in her orbit treat others, as well as the responses invited by those people's better nature. Loving legacies can even help us catch ourselves in the act when we behave in ways that run counter to the good role modeling we've received.

"My grandmother's generosity was not about showing off or proving to others how kind she was," Mike said. "Inherently, she was a sweet, loving person, and she made it emphatically clear I was a source of great joy to her. That to me is the pinnacle of generosity. She made everyone feel like they mattered."

Again, say Hello!

As I said at the start of this book, you *are* going to run into that guy—the one you think is a dick. You're going to run right into him. It's written in the stars that he's your new love interest's good pal. And that woman whose kid your child is desperate for a playdate with? Oh yeah, she thinks you're a jerk because of the time several months ago when you didn't say hi. Now you're going to have to sit next to her on a bench by a playground for the foreseeable future.

Some part of you knows, admit it, that when you smile at that person, when you take that mighty effort to be nice, you'll find out they're super kind. *They always are.*

So, go on, say hello.

ACKNOWLEDGMENTS

In many ways this book revolves around the core notion that it's very difficult to be a dick when you're in a reciprocal loving relationship with the world. As such, I thank . . .

You, Haruna Miyamoto-Borg. You challenge me every day to be a loving, generous, and kind version of myself. Waking up to love every day, loving and being loved, has been and remains the greatest inspiration for dropping the rock of dickery.

Kata and Uta, being your father is the most wonderful of all possible reasons to be whatever the opposite of a dick is. Being your *otosan* and loving you is a joy beyond measure.

By putting their trust in my care, the clients in my psychotherapy/psychoanalytic practice are among my most valuable teachers when it comes to not being a dick.

Eve Golden has been my beloved ally, source of strength, and long-time psychoanalytic editor par excellence from the very start of this process of taking experience and thought and putting it in flight.

As always, Gareth Esersky, my agent, has provided the consistent guidance and care for my work, and that of the Irrelationship Group, that undergirds this volume. Thank you, Gareth, for taking me, and for taking Danny, Grant, and I, on. Being represented by you makes me feel like the luckiest dude on earth. Working with you and the Carol Mann Agency is among the greatest gifts of this whole writing sojourn.

Pam Liflander, what can I say? You're the editorial consultant that this project required after it had chewed up and spit out several others along the way. With you, I found that elusive "good fit" between what I'd attempted to say for years and years and actually, finally, saying it.

Central Recovery Press, especially Patrick Hughes, Valerie Killeen, and Nancy Schenck, thank you! And, when push came to shove, it was Dan Hernandez who rolled up his sleeves and got into the real slog of this process with me as my editor—and comrade!—at CRP. Thanks are simply not enough, Dan. Authorship with CRP has been, as was offered when we began back in 2014, a synergistic partnership. I feel empowered by the love, care, and support that I received from you as a member of the Irrelationship project, and throughout the development of this solo endeavor.

It has been difficult, sometimes impossible, to resist acting out my inner (and not-so-inner) dick from seed to the full bloom in this project. Often, I've found that writing in a group is like being in a rock band. And now I realize that writing and publishing is always a group process. In the words of Andrew Raider Wood, the entertainment lawyer who introduced me to Gareth Esersky, "Success has many parents." Playing nice with others, and they with me, has redefined success forever for me. Not being a dick combined with the daily practice of *Satyagraha* has allowed us to dodge and parry, and survive numerous attempts to destroy the things we've come to love . . . perhaps because loving them and each other puts our hearts in such genuine peril.

The raucous band All Nite Rave was my earliest attempt to form and maintain a collaboration that was challenged to survive the clashing of egos of its many parents. Through dozens of members, it wound up being the cherished, idealized lovechild of Jim DeLozier (RIP) and I. We alone survived *it*—the original name of what Freud called "das *Id*," that raging, instinctual component of the unconscious mind that's ever at war with the ego, whose job it is to navigate consensus reality. I love you, Jim, as there is no one who sailed with me more consistently and closely toward treacherous shores. Oh, how I miss you.

Terry and Joan DeLozier. The world is not the same without Jim and I'm disoriented in ways I continue to discover. The love and refuge you gave us Corona del Mar punks still lives inside me.

Outside of my marriage, my relationships with Dr. Grant Brenner and Danny Berry via the Irrelationship Project represent the most contemporary shape my aspiration toward collaboration has taken. While we're not all comfortable with me comparing this project to a marriage, I can say it remains among my most rewarding experiences. Thanks guys.

Matt Stedman, for the calming, nurturing counsel on our surf sojourns up and down the East Coast. Cowabunga, dude!

James Rogers. Who knew oceanography would open my heart and mind to the adventures of learning? I thank you from the bottom of my heart for seeing what you saw and not giving up.

Also, thank you, Dr. Jeanne Henry for taking me under your wing at Newport Harbor Adolescent Psychiatric Hospital, showing me the ropes, and opening the door to the vast, amazing field of mental health care. Thank you, Dr. Ronda Hampton, my professional soul mate, for the years of shoulder-to-shoulder camaraderie on the front lines of community crisis intervention in Avalon Gardens, South Central Los Angeles. Dr. Maggie Decker, I'm so grateful for your guidance, care, love, and supervision at AIDS Service Foundation in the mid 1990s. These three experiences have formed the central core of my professional identity and I carry you with me every day through what often feels like *clinical mayhem.* I love this work, and you three have made that possible.

PR *par excellence,* Kelli Daniel of Dart Frogg—you rock!

Thank you, Charlotte Rolland for giving me a consistent love that proved itself in action. I believe all these years since you've been gone sets the cornerstone of my willingness and ability to love and be loved.

Thank you, Charlotte and Jon Rysanek. Hope you read this book even though it might be hard to get past the title. Fixing what was broken between us has been among the most miraculous examples of what love can do. I'm so grateful for the love we share, and so happy for the love shared between my beloved Grrrrrrrls—Haruna, Kata, and Uta—and their Nana and Papa.

Thank you, Sandy Borg for an excellent evening of lion-taming. Its benefits express themselves in my life every day. And thanks Erik Borg for *also* loving me through all that.

Love and gratitude to you, Mark Borg and Bonnie Mankoff. Your steady thoughtfulness and kindness maintain our connection across miles and years.

I'm deeply grateful for Osamu and Yoko Miyamoto. I love you, and I believe I hit the jackpot in the in-law department. *Arigato gozaimasu* for all the love and generosity you consistently shower upon your NYC family no matter the geographic distance.

Wil Diaz, what in the world would I do without our early morning walks in the East Village?! Much, much love, man!

Cheers to the snarling wolverines in the back row, especially you, Ronnie Sawyer and Mary Jane Rambo!

Special mention (again) to those mods and punks, surfers, shrinks, black sheep, iconoclasts, colleagues, mentors, supervisors, and soul mates who, from a vast array of time periods and contexts, have loved and were loved by me in ways that still fuel a wider and ever-expanding *raison d'être*. Special thanks to: Greg Hex, Bill Defina, Britt Huycke, Karin Nance, Phil Vock, Megan Hardy, Byron Abel, Robert Taube, Glenn Parish, Paul Loringer, Steve Torrey, Scott Murdock, Cheo Rodriguez, Liz Rusch, Eric Lee, Marty Strom, Emily Garrod, Mik Manenti, Stuart Pyle, Marcus Ho, Susan Greenfield, Tom Cox, Emily Damron-Cox, Paco and Maiken Lozano-Wiese, Rob Gutfliesh, Helmut Krackie, Scott Graham, James Kwon, Pat Kenary, Bobbi Fuentes, Rie Ogura, James Gary, Sr., Machiko Makabe, David Kopstein, Scott Stewart, Tim Barnes, Mark Lanaghan, Adrian Sutton, Molly Goldman, Valentina McFarland, Ilene Segalove, Dave Jawor, Gloria Robotham, Elizabeth Shanahan, Jan Healy, Isa Stanfels, John Henry Eldridge, Norman Karns, Shawn Marie Turi, John Hatchett, Daniel Leyva, Michael Lynch, Maureen Kamsi-Storey, Joerg Bose, Sandra Buechler, Jack Drescher, Sue Kolod, Brent Willock, Jack Eppler, Kako Takeuchi, Zeke and Sheila Zimmerman, John Flikeid, Connie Rolland, Jules Cohen, Hara Estroff-Marano, Ilene Segalove, John Ellert, Scott Munsey, Jennifer McCarroll, Chana Pollack, Myra Mniewski, Matt Dalton, Elise Cox, Sheila McManus, Ilene Mykoliw, Ray Curran, Stuart Lachs, Mike Moore, Barry Williams, Ken Robidoux, Mauri Helffrich, David Lester, Gary Ireland, Ruthann Starkey-Shipley, Karl Bateman, John Lance Harrison, Amy Kerr, Tim Couch, Sean

Carver, Wendy and Kim Marshall, Paul Tully, Daniel MacNamee, and Brendan Rafferty. In the immortal words of Jim Carroll, "I salute you brother[s]"—and sisters!

NOTES

1. It is possible that the word "dick" has much more universal applications—as the book, *How Not to Be a Dick*, was written by a woman, and the female inmates at Litchfield Prison in *Orange Is the New Black* regularly use the term in reference to each other. Also, Aaron James (2012) suggests that some slurs are gendered—e.g., asshole is male, bitch is female. Though dick is still open, ironically, gender-wise (p. 90).

2. I see things in thoroughly relational terms (e.g., *Irrelationship* and *Relationship Sanity*) and find that there are many times (especially in romantic relationships and family systems) where one person takes ALL the blame for things that are related to the system itself (the couple or the family). The family therapists call this "identified patient"—and it is relevant to our study of dicks in systems.

3. See Borg, Brenner & Berry (2015, 2018) for an overview and analysis of how we jointly create psychological defense systems to protect ourselves from the very things that we "want" from long-term love.

4. DeMello, Anthony. *Awareness: The Perils and Opportunities of Reality.* New York: Image, 1990, p.5

5. See Borg (2010) from a detailed overview, description, and analysis of character as the "sum total of psychological defense" (p. 22).

6. Sullivan, Harry Stack. *The Interpersonal Theory of Psychiatry.* New York: W. W. Norton, 1953, p.158.

7. Sullivan, Harry Stack. *The Interpersonal Theory of Psychiatry.* New York: W. W. Norton, 1953, pp. 178–182.

[8] Though the term enactment is a contemporary psychoanalytic concept that goes well beyond the scope of this book, it is necessary to give a brief definition to help understand the community dynamics explored in this chapter. One approach to understanding transference-countertransference interactions is by analyzing patient-analyst enactments. Irwin Hirsch defines these as "what happens when the analyst unwittingly actualizes the patient's transference and, together with the patient, lives out [the] intrapsychic configurations . . . [enactment] is viewed as the patient's unconscious effort to persuade or force the analyst into a reciprocal action: a two-party playing out of the patient's most fundamental internalized configurations" (Hirsch, 1998, p. 78). Similarly, Edgar Levenson believes that change in a system is created through a practitioner's "ability to be trapped, immersed, and participating in the system and then work his [or her] way out" (Levenson, 1972, p. 174). In its broadest sense, the enactment concept can also be used to describe and address how all interactions—in analysis as well as in our daily lives—are tainted by the unconscious dynamics of the enactors. This raises the question of whether enactments are so ubiquitous in our daily lives as to be increasingly useless (at least as special cases of unconscious material) in analytic settings. From this perspective, Lewis Aron (2003) asserts that "we are correct to ask, 'What is *not* an enactment?'" (p. 623). However, he goes on to suggest that enactments "may well be a central means by which patients and analysts enter into each other's inner world and discover themselves as participants within each other's psychic life, mutually constructing the relational matrix that constitutes the medium of psychoanalysis" (Ibid., p. 629).

[9] Klein, Melanie. "Notes on Some Schizoid Mechanisms." *International Journal Psycho-Analysis*, 27 (1946): 99–110.

[10] Rycoft, Charles Frederick. *A Critical Dictionary of Psychoanalysis.* New York: Penguin, 1995.

[11] Freud, Sigmund. "Remembering, Repeating and Working Through." In *The Standard Edition of the Complete Psychological Works of Sigmund Freud, Vol. 12*, translated and edited by James Strachey, 145-156. London: The Hogarth Press, 1914, p. 150.

¹² Freud, Sigmund. "Fragment of an Analysis of a Case of Hysteria." *The Standard Edition of the Complete Psychological Works of Sigmund Freud, Vol. 7* translated and edited by James Strachey, 3-122. London: The Hogarth Press, 1901, p. 119.

¹³ Lacan, Jacques. *The Four Fundamental Concepts of Psychoanalysis.* New York: W. W. Norton, 1998.

¹⁴ Slavoj Žižek. *The Parallax View.* Cambridge, MA: MIT Press, 2006.

¹⁵ Borg, Jr., Mark B. "Venturing Beyond the Consulting Room: Psychoanalysis in Community Crisis Intervention. *Contemporary Psychoanalysis,* 40 no. 2 (2004): 147-174.

¹⁶ In behavioral probability statistics, regression toward the mean is the tendency for scores—and/or behaviors—to average out. The idea is that we typically revert to our average, expectable way of being.

¹⁷ Alcoholics Anonymous World Services. *Alcoholics Anonymous.* New York: AA World Services. Inc, 1997

¹⁸ Emotion is associated with mood, temperament, personality, and disposition. The English word "emotion" is derived from the French word *émouvoir.* This is based on the Latin *emovere,* where *e-* (variant of *ex-*) means "out" and *movere* means "move". The related term "motivation" is also derived from *movere.*

No definitive taxonomy of emotions exists, though numerous taxonomies have been proposed. Some categorizations include:

- "Cognitive" versus "non-cognitive" emotions
- Instinctual emotions (from the amygdala), versus cognitive emotions (from the prefrontal cortex).
- Basic versus complex: Where base emotions lead to more complex ones.
- Categorization based on duration: Some emotions occur over a period of seconds (e.g. surprise) where others can last years (e.g. love).

A related distinction is between the emotion and the results of the emotion, principally behaviors and emotional expressions. People often behave in certain ways as a direct result of their emotional state, such as crying, fighting, or fleeing. Yet again, if one can have the emotion without the corresponding behavior then we may consider the behavior not to be essential to the emotion. Neuroscientific research suggests there is a "magic quarter second" during which it's possible to catch a thought before it becomes an emotional reaction. In that instant, one can catch a feeling before allowing it to take hold.

The James-Lange theory posits that emotional experience is largely due to the experience of bodily changes. The functionalist approach to emotions (e.g., Nico-Frijda) holds that emotions have evolved for a particular function, such as to keep the subject safe.

[19] Sullivan Harry Stack. *The Interpersonal Theory of Psychiatry*. New York: Norton, 1953.

[20] Freud, Sigmund. "Mourning and melancholia." *The Standard Edition of the Complete Psychological Works of Sigmund Freud, 14*, translated and edited by James Strachey, 237-258. London: Hogarth Press, 1917.

[21] Dissociation, from an interpersonal perspective, can manifest as depression—and can be counted among those "things" that can alleviate our conscious experience of anxiety (Bose, 1995, 1998).

[22] Ainsworth, Mary. "The Development of Infant-Mother Attachment." In B. Cardwell & H. Ricciuti (Eds.) *Review of Child Development Research* (Vol. 3, pp. 1-94) Chicago: University of Chicago Press, 1973; Bowlby John. *Attachment and Loss: Vol. 1*. New York: Basic Books, 1969.

[23] Bowlby, John. "The Nature of the Child's Tie to His Mother." *International Journal of Psychoanalysis, 39*, 350-371, 1958.

[24] Dan Siegel, 1999, *The Developing Mind*, p. 26.

[25] Chua, Amy. *Battle Hymn of the Tiger Mother*. New York: Penguin, 2011.

[26] Chua, Amy. "Why Chinese Mothers are Superior." *Wall Street Journal* (1/08/2011).

[27] Estroff Marano, Hara. *Nation of Wimps: The High Cost of Invasive Parenting*. New York: Crown Archetype, 2008.

28 When this kind of a dynamic plays out in therapy, shrinks see it as a meeting of the patterns of interaction that clients unconsciously bring forward and repeat in current relationships (transference) and those that the therapist brings and repeats in interaction from her or his own history (countertransference). When that meeting occurs in therapy, we call it *enactment*. Enactment is the way that our old and unresolved relationship dynamics manifest and are played out in contemporary relationships—and they provide an opportunity for them to be seen, addressed, and worked through (i.e., changed).

29 This section was inspired by and adapted from an exceptional article titled "Catharsis" by David McRaney from the 8/11/2011 *You Are Not So Smart: A Celebration of Self-Delusion* blog (https:// youarenotsosmart.com/2010/08/11/catharsis/).

30 Ibid., 2011.

31 Psychologist Brad Bushman at Iowa State decided to study whether or not venting actually worked. Freud's long shadow still tyrannized the landscape when it came to conventional wisdom on "getting the anger out," and the prevailing advice when it came to dealing with stress and anger was to punch inanimate objects and scream into pillows.

Bushman, like many psychologists before him, felt like this might be bad advice. In one of Bushman's (2002) studies he divided 180 students into three groups.

1. One group read a neutral article.

2. One group read an article about a fake study that said venting anger was effective.

3. The third group read about a fake study that said venting was pointless.

Bushman then had the students write essays for or against abortion, a subject for which he assumed they'd have strong feelings. He told them that their essays would be graded by fellow students—they weren't.

When they got their essays back, half were told their essay was superb. The other half had this scrawled across the paper: "This is one of the worst essays I have ever read!" They then asked the subjects to pick an activity like play a game, watch some comedy, read a story, or punch a bag.

What happened?

The people who read the article that said venting worked, and who later got angry, were far more likely to ask to punch the bag than those who got angry in the other groups. In all the groups, the people who got praised tended to pick non-aggressive activities (reported by David McRaney, 2011).

32 Bushman, Brad J. "Does Venting Anger Feed or Extinguish the Flame? Catharsis, Rumination, Distraction, Anger, and Aggressive Responding. *Personality and Social Psychology Bulletin*, 28 no. 6 (2002): 724-731.

33 Frank Lachmann (2000) addresses ways that this plays out in clinical treatment in his amazing book, *Transforming Aggression: Psychotherapy with the Difficult-to-Treat Patient.*

34 My wife, Haruna, and I published an in-depth analysis of this stage of relationship development: "The Borderline Stage of Relationship." *Psychology Research*, 2 no. 1 (2012): 1-13.

35 Greene, Robert. *The 48 Laws of Power*. New York: Penguin, p. ix, 2000, p. ix.

36 Paraphrased from the "Tools of Chapter 9"—Couples in Recovery Anonymous.

37 Doherty, Meghan, *How Not To Be A Dick: An Everyday Etiquette Guide*, Zest Books, San Francisco, CA, 2013, p. 12.

38 Beattie, Melody. *Codependent No More: How to Stop Controlling Others and Start Caring for Yourself*. Center City, MN: Hazelden, 1986, p. 209.

39 A reference to 12&12 *Step Four*, "Our present anxieties and troubles, we cry, are caused by the behavior of other people—people who really need a moral inventory" (p. 45).

40 Tronick, E. Z. & Gianino, A. F. (1986). Interactive mismatch and repair: Challenges to the coping infant. *Zero to Three, 6*, 1-6.

BIBLIOGRAPHY

Ainsworth, Mary. "The Development of Infant-Mother Attachment. In Bettye Cardwell & Henry N. Ricciuti (Eds.) *Review of Child Development Research* (Vol. 3, pp. 1-94) Chicago: University of Chicago Press, 1973.

Alcoholics Anonymous World Services. *Alcoholics Anonymous.* New York: Alcoholics Anonymous World Services, Inc., 1997.

Alcoholics Anonymous World Services. *Twelve Steps and Twelve Traditions.* New York: AA World Services, Inc., 2002.

Aron, Lewis. "The Paradoxical Place of Enactment in Psychoanalysis." *Psychoanalytic Dialogues, 13* (2003): 623-632.

Beattie, Melody. *Codependent No More: How to Stop Controlling Others and Start Caring for Yourself.* Center City, MN: Hazelden, 1986.

Beckett, Samuel. *Worstward Ho.* New York: Grove Press, 1984.

Belford, David. "Breaks in the Flow: The Role of Repair in the Attachment Relationship." http://www.cdd.unm.edu/ecln/hvt/common/pdfs/2011_11.pdf, 2011.

Bennett, Michael I. and Bennett, Sarah, *F*ck Feelings: One Shrink's Practical Advice For Managing All Life's Impossible Problems*, Simon & Schuster, New York, 2015

Borg, Jr., Mark B. "Venturing Beyond the Consulting Room: Psychoanalysis in Community Crisis Intervention. *Contemporary Psychoanalysis, 40* no. 2 (2004): 147-174.

Borg, Jr., Mark B. "Community Psychoanalysis: Developing a Model of Psychoanalytically-Informed Community Crisis Intervention." In Niklas Lange and Marie Wagner (Eds.) *Community Psychology: New Directions* (pp. 1-66). Hauppauge, NY: Nova Science Publishers, 2010.

Borg, Jr., Mark. B., Grant H. Brenner, and Daniel Berry. *Irrelationship: How We Use Dysfunctional Relationships to Hide from Intimacy.* Las Vegas, NV: Central Recovery Press, 2015.

Borg, Jr., Mark B., Grant H. Brenner, and Daniel Berry. *Relationship Sanity: Creating and Maintaining Healthy Relationships.* Las Vegas, NV: Central Recovery Press, 2018.

Borg, Jr., Mark B., and Haruna Miyamoto-Borg. "The Borderline Stage of Relationship." *Psychology Research,* 2 no. 1 (2012): 1-13.

Bose, Joerg. "Trauma, Depression, and Mourning." *Contemporary Psychoanalysis* 31, no. 3 (1995): 399-407.

Bose, Joerg. "The Inhumanity of the Other: Treating Trauma and Depression." *The Review of Interpersonal Psychoanalysis* 3, no. 1 (1998): 1-4.

Bowlby, John. "The Nature of the Child's Tie to His Mother." *International Journal of Psychoanalysis,* 39, 350-371, 1958. Bowlby John. *Attachment and Loss: Vol. 1.* New York: Basic Books, 1969.

Bushman, Brad J. "Does Venting Anger Feed or Extinguish the Flame? Catharsis, Rumination, Distraction, Anger, and Aggressive Responding. *Personality and Social Psychology Bulletin,* 28 no. 6 (2002): 724-731.

Chua, Amy. *Battle Hymn of the Tiger Mother.* New York: Penguin, 2011.

Chua, Amy. "Why Chinese Mothers are Superior." *Wall Street Journal* (1/08/2011).

Chua, Amy. "The Tiger Mother Responds to Readers." *Wall Street Journal* (1/13/2011).

DeMello, Anthony. *Awareness.* New York: Image, 1990.

Doherty, Meghan, *How Not To Be A Dick: An Everyday Etiquette Guide*, Zest Books, San Francisco, CA, 2013.

Estroff Marano, Hara. *Nation of Wimps: The High Cost of Invasive Parenting*. New York: Crown Archetype, 2008.

Fairbairn, William Ronald Dodds. *Psychological Studies of the Personality*. London: Routledge & Kegan Paul, 1952.

Freud, Sigmund. "Remembering, Repeating and Working Through." In *The Standard Edition of the Complete Psychological Works of Sigmund Freud, Vol. 12*, translated and edited by James Strachey, 145- 156. London: The Hogarth Press, 1914.

Freud, Sigmund. "Mourning and melancholia." *The Standard Edition of the Complete Psychological Works of Sigmund Freud, 14*, translated and edited by James Strachey, 237-258. London: Hogarth Press, 1917.

Gottman, John S., & Gottman, Julie M. *10 Principles for Doing Effective Couples Therapy*. New York: Norton, 2015.

Greene, Robert. *The 48 Laws of Power*. New York: Penguin, 2000.

Hirsch, Irwin. "The Concept of Enactment and Theoretical Convergence." *Psychoanalytic Quarterly*, 67 (1998): 78-101.

James, Aaron. *Assholes: A Theory*. New York: Anchor Books, 2012.

Klein, Melanie. "Notes on Some Schizoid Mechanisms.". *International Journal Psycho-Analysis*, 27 (1946):99-110.

Lacan, Jacques. *The Four Fundamental Concepts of Psychoanalysis*. New York: W. W. Norton, 1998.

Lachmann, Frank M. *Transforming Aggression: Psychotherapy with the Difficult-to-Treat Patient*. Lanham, MD: Rowman & Littlefield Publishers, 2000.

Levenson, Edgar. *The Fallacy of Understanding*. New York: Basic Books, 1972.

McRaney, David. Catharsis. *You Are Not So Smart: A Celebration of Self-Delusion* blog (https://youarenotsosmart.com/2010/08/11/catharsis/), 2011. Downloaded 8/8/2017.

Rycoft, Charles. *A Critical Dictionary of Psychoanalysis*. New York: Penguin, 1995.

Siegel, Dan J. *The Developing Mind: Toward a Neurobiology of Interpersonal Experience*. New York: Guilford Press, 1999.

Sullivan, Harry Stack. *The Interpersonal Theory of Psychiatry*. New York: W. W. Norton, 1953.

Tronick, Edward Z. "Emotions and Emotional Communication in Infants." *American Psychologist*, 44 (1989):112–119.

Tronick, E. Z. & Gianino, A. F. (1986). Interactive mismatch and repair: Challenges to the coping infant. Zero to Three, 6, 1-6.

Žižek, Slavoj. *The Parallax View*. Cambridge, MA: MIT Press, 2006.

ABOUT THE AUTHOR

Mark B. Borg, Jr., PhD, is a community psychologist and psychoanalyst, founding partner of The Community Consulting Group, and a supervisor of psychotherapy at the William Alanson White Institute. He has written extensively about the intersection of psychoanalysis and community crisis intervention. He has been in private practice in New York City since 1998. Dr. Borg attended graduate school at the California School of Professional Psychology, where he earned both his MA and PhD in a dual-track program in clinical and community psychology. While there, Dr. Borg served on a four-year community empowerment project that was developed in South Central Los Angeles in the wake of the 1992 riots. Also at that time, he conducted individual and group psychotherapy at the AIDS Services Foundation in Orange County, California. Dr. Borg is the co-author of *Irrelationship: How We Use Dysfunctional Relationships to Hide from Intimacy* and its follow-up book, *Relationship Sanity: Creating and Maintaining Healthy Relationships.*

Printed in the USA
CPSIA information can be obtained
at www.ICGtesting.com
JSHW022322140824
68134JS00019B/1246